Everything You Ever Wanted to Know About Social Media,

but were afraid to ask...

Building Your Business
Using Consumer Generated Media

HILARY JM TOPPER, MPA

iUniverse, Inc.
New York   Bloomington

Everything You Ever Wanted to Know About
Social Media, but were afraid to ask...
Building Your Business Using Consumer Generated Media

iUniverse books may be ordered through booksellers or by contacting:

iUniverse
1663 Liberty Drive
Bloomington, IN 47403
www.iuniverse.com
1-800-Authors (1-800-288-4677)

Because of the dynamic nature of the Internet, any Web
addresses or links contained in this book may have changed
since publication and may no longer be valid.

ISBN: 978-1-4401-5362-4 (pbk)
ISBN: 978-1-4401-5364-8 (cloth)
ISBN: 978-1-4401-5363-1 (ebk)

Library of Congress Control Number: 2009931627

Printed in the United States of America

iUniverse rev. date: 7/6/2009

Cover Designed by HJMT COMMUNICATIONS, LLC

This book is dedicated to my family, staff, friends and my entire online community.

Contents

Preface

I've been a public relations practitioner for nearly 30 years. I started my career as an intern at Public I Publicity in New York City, where I worked on entertainment clients. The following year, I worked at Clairol, Inc. in the PR department and interned at Ogilvy & Mather PR/NY. After graduating from Hunter College in 1984, both positions offered me jobs. I decided to take the Ogilvy & Mather PR position. There I worked on many different accounts including DOVE Beauty Bar and Kinder-Care Learning Centers. When Hill, Holliday, Connors, Cosmopolous/PR opened their NY office, the CEO asked my boss and I to start up the firm's public relations department.

After that, I decided to try something different. I landed a job at Altro Health and Rehabilitation Services and I worked there for many years. Altro was a non-profit organization dedicated to helping people with psychiatric disabilities get job training and job placement. I started as the coordinator of public relations and later become director of public relations and development. The year that Altro merged with Federated Employment and Guidance Services (FEGS), I decided to go back into the private sector and landed a job at Ruder Finn/

PR. There, I worked on the Jell-O, GLAD Wrap and Bags and other consumer product accounts.

I was weaned back into the non-profit sector when a friend, who I had worked with at Altro, told me about another opportunity in Queens. I decided to take him up on the offer and worked as the public relations/development director at PSCH.

About a year later, I became pregnant with my daughter and decided that the time was right to start HJMT COMMUNICATIONS, LLC. I started the firm in March 1992 with a phone and computer. I slowly built up my client base and eventually moved the family out of an apartment into a house, where we converted the garage into an office. A few years went by and having seven employees in my house all the time didn't thrill me so we moved to a suite in Long Beach, New York.

After the first year, I met Kristie Galvani. She became employed as my office manager. (Now, she is Senior VP of the firm.) About two years after that, I hired Lori Alexy, who is now the VP of Client Services. When the five-year lease was up for renewal, we strategically decided to move to Westbury, which was more centrally located on Long Island. By doing so, we tripled in staff and tripled in revenue.

Today, we are a small boutique firm employing 10 full-timers and a handful of part-timers. We represent large businesses, small companies and non-profit organizations by helping them with publicity, social media, event planning and graphic design.

About three years ago in November 2006, Lisa Gordon who runs my Rochester office and I attended a Critical Issues Forum in New York City for the Council of Public Relations Firms. The discussion focused on Twitter, Blogging, Microblogging, Facebook, Podcasts and more. I walked out of the event shaking my head.

"How could this take off?" I thought.

About a month later, my son decided to put me on Facebook as a joke to get his older sister angry. My first friends were Marcelle Fischler of the *New York Times*, Jamie Herzlich of *Newsday* and Adina Genn of *Long Island Business News*.

That's when I realized that social media was much bigger than I originally thought. I read all the books I could on the subject and followed key bloggers to learn as much as possible and realized that there was a gap. The one book I couldn't find on the shelves was a basic social media 101 book that reviewed a variety of social networking sites and offered an understanding about how to use these sites to build a business. That is why I put my efforts into developing this book. I wanted to educate people about social media, understand the power of consumer-generated media and use it to help their business grow.

I hope you get a lot out of this book and my door is always open for questions. You can email me at hilary@hjmt.com, friend me on all the social media sites mentioned in this book at Hilary Topper or Hiltop25 and you can follow me on Twitter at @Hilary25.

Introduction

More than 1.5 billion people use Twitter, 150 billion have a Facebook page and billions of people view YouTube videos everyday. That's not all. There are thousands of social networking sites on the Internet, including specialized community groups. With these types of numbers growing daily, it's no wonder our communication methods are changing. But are we communicating our messages effectively? Or, are messages lost in a nonstop stream of endless chatter? Or worse, are we standing by the sidelines watching while competitors successfully reap the benefits of everything social media has to offer?

Gone are the days of our reliance on the U.S. Postal Service, the telephone and the fax to send our messages. Today, everything is different. Businesses organizations and even individuals now rely on social networking sites, blogs and online tools to spread the word about a product, service or company. Done right, social media is crucial in getting a message and brand out to a target audience. It increases awareness and also maintains visibility in the public's eye.

Social media used to be primarily for kids and teens. The millennium population has enjoyed MySpace, Facebook and YouTube for years. Social networking is a natural way for them to communicate with each other like the way the rest of us used the telephone growing up. Social media is an extension of what the next generation of consumers will expect from all businesses.

The influence of social media grows daily. Consumers believe their friends and neighbors when friends and neighbors endorse a product or service, frequent a restaurant or believe in a cause. Social media is also called conversational media or consumer-generated media. A message spreads from one friend to another to another and another until it spreads throughout the Internet. This is called viral marketing.

The power of social media will continue to grow as time goes by. Large companies like, JetBlue Airlines, Whole Foods, Dell Computer and so on, have already embraced the new media. By doing so, their market share has significantly increased.

These corporations and thought leaders are now paving the way for smaller businesses. Consider following the leaders, note their conversations and emulate what seems to be successful. It is also important to stay true to yourself and your company and be as transparent as possible.

With the downturn economy, the housing market at an all time low, major daily newspapers closing their doors every day, the automobile industry on the verge of bankruptcy and jobs being sent oversees, who knows who will be left standing once everything turns around. But one thing seems certain, consumer generated media enables businesses to engage their customer base, build a loyal following and manage their reputations. It enables businesses to learn more about their customers and form solid relationships.

For so many years, we have lived in a society where we have been anonymous. In a world where no one knows anything about anyone else and for a long time, we liked it that way. Social media is a way to replace what technology wiped out -- the personal touch.

Perhaps it's just a way of getting back to the small village (pre-technology, pre-automobile) way before the advent of the box store, when you knew the owner of the general store, who he was, what kind of family he had and where he came from.

Isn't it time that we started to know and care about each other on a real business level instead of a superficial business level? Isn't that what customer service is all about?

Where Have We Been?

"If Facebook was really counting friends, there would never be trouble finding enough poker players for Thursdays nights or finding enough players for basketball games."

Guillermo Paz, Director Comercial
Infoxel de Argentina S.A.

* * *

Close your eyes and think back to when you were young. Do you remember what technology you had in your house?

Growing up, I had a black and white television in my parent's bedroom with no remote and a single telephone that we kept in the kitchen. As technology became more affordable, I remember my parents buying a color television set. We were the first in the neighborhood to have a color set and my friends were so jealous!

After that, we started to have phones in all of the rooms in our home and eventually, my parents offered my older sister, Lori, her own phone number. That was a *big* deal. Everyone wanted his or her own phone line, Lori included.

My parents had a Super 8 camera that recorded on film that we played back on a projector. I remember sitting in the living room watching the movies we made on a roll up screen.

In the 1970s, the Polaroid Land camera was the next big breakthrough in technology. It was amazing because it had film that developed within seconds. (Fanning the photos was half the fun!) Everyone wanted one. It was the hottest product around. Unfortunately, I remember the film being very expensive and when my parents bought a Polaroid camera for the house, they controlled every photo we took.

We also had a record player that played 45s, 78s and regular LPs. My friends and I compared albums while listening to music. Lori was a big music listener too. My fondest memory was when she played her favorite songs over and over and over again, in order to learn the words. She favored Earth, Wind and Fire, Carole King and America. I liked the heavier sound of The Who, Rolling Stones and Led Zeppelin.

Before I graduated high school, the first Sony Walkman appeared on the market. People listened to music through headphones and loved the portability of the product. My friends and I snuck our Walkmans into high school but couldn't listen until we were outside during recess or lunch, out of the teacher's sight.

When I went to college and lived in New York City, the Discman was the music device of choice. It was unbelievable! Compact disks fit into tiny little players and we played our favorite CD while wandering through town. I walked around New York City listening to "Talking Heads 77" on my Discman. I played it over and over again because I only brought along one CD.

In the mid 1980s, I worked at Ogilvy & Mather PR. We had a telex machine that allowed us to send documents internationally. This machine was so big that it needed a room of its own! Each desk had an IBM typewriter with correction ribbon and if you made a typo, all you had to do was press the back space key on your keyboard to erase it. For massive changes, you used white out or strips of white out and would type over it after it dried. I remember working until 11pm trying to make sure that every line and every word looked as perfect as possible and that the white out did its job.

A few months into my first job, management announced everyone in the organization was getting a word processor. I remember the other assistant account executives getting upset. I was mad too!

"If we learn word-processing, then we will never be able to move up," my friend Sheila told me, upset that we would be forever stuck in our current position, when we were capable of so much more.

"I worked too hard in college to be a secretary for the rest of my life," said my friend Nancy.

Of course that wasn't the case. Having a word processor made it so much easier to edit. Instead of staying until 11pm, we finished our work by 9:30pm.

I even remember the first Macintosh computer. It was so incredibly cool. It was a small little box-shaped machine that sat on your desk. It had a graphic user interface complete with smiley Mac and dogcow (that made "moof" sounds). The Mac could do so much and you didn't even need to know basic computer language to use it. Shortly thereafter, computers became ubiquitous. Businesses had computers and so did families. Computers became smaller and more compact.

In the 1980s, my husband, Brian, worked at Westlaw, a provider of legal research services. He trained other attorneys on the Westlaw system and conducted legal research. I was amazed at all the information at his fingertips. He could find out so much with the click of a few buttons. I never realized that technology would continue expanding at such a rapid pace.

In the late 1980s early 1990s, mobile phones came on to the market. At first, you only saw them in people's cars. (I think my father-in-law was one of the first to have one.) Then you saw people with them on the streets. Those chatting on phones while walking looked as if they held a loaf of bread to their ear! My friends and I supposed those calls must be very important. "Why wouldn't someone wait until they got to a pay phone to make a call?" we asked each other.

Today, there are very few pay phones around. (I know, because I left my cell phone at home one time and had to find one. Little did I know the old charge of 25 cents for a call doubled to 50 cents!) Now, everyone has a cell phone, including children and senior citizens and many use these phones as their primary number.

Within the past 10 years, the trend has been to text message, that is, short message service or SMS, instead of talk. I find myself regularly sending out quick text messages, preferring to do that than call someone. When I had a Blackberry, I used Blackberry Messenger to send out messages. It worked similar to Instant Messenger, which my staff and I use in my office to communicate with each other.

When I started HJMT COMMUNICATIONS, LLC, the full-service boutique public relations, event planning, social media and graphic design agency in March 1992 out of my one bedroom apartment in Long Beach, NY, I had a rotary telephone and an Apple computer. That was all I needed!

Today, I have three offices – Westbury, Manhattan and Rochester and all I need is a telephone (my iPhone) and a computer (my laptop). The one thing that has changed is I now communicate via social networking sites. I talk with my parents, friends, clients and business associates all on Facebook (see Chapter 9), LinkedIn (see Chapter 16), Plaxo (see Chapter 17), Twitter (see Chapter 21), Brightkite (see Chapter 6), Seesmic (see Chapter 5) and FriendFeed (see Chapter 11). And, I'm coordinating with my staff on Yammer (see Chapter 22).

In addition to communicating via emails and instant messages, I also use Skype (a computer program you can use to talk with people through live video) and even blogs. Sometimes, it all seems too distracting. And yet, if you think back to simpler eras, our communication method was just as distracting. You would be in the middle of some task and the phone or doorbell would ring. Times are changing and we need to change with them to find that perfect balance in our lives as technology continues to evolve.

In the following chapters, we will explore the world of social media, putting it into context to enhance productivity, expand social reach and understand and appreciate its value in today's technological world. Subsequent chapters will focus on how to build business using social media tools. All of the opinions stated in this book are either the sole opinions of the author or my online community.

At the end of each chapter, I added "My 2 Cents" to analyze and evaluate the site to help you cut through the clutter.

The Basics

"To paraphrase Jon Stewart, "new" does not always equal
"good." Companies and individuals need to fully evaluate and
understand new technologies before adoption. Observe how other
people use a tool/service before you jump in. And don't be afraid
to ask your kids about how all this newfangled stuff works!"

Julie Dickenson, Research Director
Rochester Business Journal

*   *   *

Why bother with social media? What can be gained from it?

Many people tell me that they feel that social media is just a "waste of time" and that there is just too much clutter. What people don't realize is that social media is becoming the fastest way to communicate ideas and values, even faster than word of mouth because social media creates viral marketing.

Just look around. Everyday, there is another article from a government agency, corporation or small business using social media sites to get their word out. For example, I was at my parent's home in Tamarac, Florida and was reading the *TamAgram*, the official publication of the city of Tamarac, Florida. The lead story was "Tweet, Tweet! We're on Twitter, You Should Be Too!" The story talked about how the city is using Twitter to send information to its residents.

If municipalities are using social media to get their message across and if corporations are using it to promote their products and services, then don't you think you can promote your business this way too?

You have taken the first step by purchasing this book and now you will learn to promote your goods and services via social media.

And Now The Real Basics

While writing this book, I realized that there are a lot of new terms to know and understand prior to delving into social media. This chapter provides the basics, while subsequent chapters will reinforce what you learn here and show you how to use it in concrete ways.

Building a Community

Is the basis for all social media. The goal is to gather people who have similar interests or ideals and bring them together to form a community or, what Seth Godin in his book, *Tribes*, calls a tribe.

Social Networking Sites

Online places where you build communities and exchange

dialog with that community. All social networking sites are very similar. Most feature a place to post your status (or what you are currently doing) and on this status, you can have conversations with your friends and followers (defined below). You also have an opportunity to post photos and videos and you can share a little bit about your personal life to help make a connection.

Friends and Followers

People in your social networking community. Each social networking site calls these people something different. For example, on Facebook, they are called friends, on LinkedIn, they are called contacts, on Plaxo, they are called connections and on Twitter, they are called followers.

Blogs

Weblogs or online diaries. Some bloggers (writers of blogs) talk about their personal lives or businesses while others blog about specific topics. There are industry-related blogs, for example, blogs about social media and marketing. There are blogs about niche markets like fishing, golfing, running, dieting and more. Blogs also help build a community by creating interesting posts where people can comment and get a conversation started.

Microblogs

Mini blogs (or more commonly known as status updates) that have only 140 characters. Some people microblog about what they are doing, promoting or need that day. Others microblog to promote their blogs. Examples of people who microblog and blog include important policy makers like President Barack

Obama who uses this to build a consensus for his agenda; celebrities like Britney Spears to build a fan base; and large corporations like Dunkin' Donuts and Starbucks to build their brand.

Link Shrinking

Software like Tiny URL and Adjix are used to shrink long URL's that you can then use in the microblog. Go to either site, paste in the long URL, click on the link and then you will be provided with a shorter version. With only 140 characters allowed, make sure every character counts. By shrinking your URL, you can fit more content into your microblog. (Many of the new features on some of the social networking sites automatically shrink the URL, so you may not have to take this extra step.)

Real Simple Syndication (RSS)

Allows you to receive information via news or feed aggregator like Bloglines or iGoogle. Both takes all of the RSS feeds and puts them in one place. This enables you to read blogs that you are following all in one location. You can also send RSS feeds to your email address, which is another convenient way to compile them into one place.

Wikis

Web pages that allow individuals to update or add information to the page. For example, Wikipedia is the online encyclopedia that enables anyone to input information on just about anything. Wikipedia has become the online source to get free information.

Years ago, it was Encyclopedia Britannica, now it's Wikipedia, written by consumers like you.

An Internet Forum or Online Message Board

Where people with common interests get together and post messages. Questions are asked and answered by those involved in similar situations, in a non-real time discussion group.

Chat Rooms

Places where people go to find others with common interests. There are many different types of chat rooms including ones on AOL and Yahoo. To find a list of various chat rooms on the Internet, search a specific topic and various chat rooms will come up on the search engine. The difference between chat rooms and forums or message boards is that they take place in real time getting you instantaneous responses.

Listserv

Similar to a chat room or a forum. Listservs enables you to join a group or community and post questions or comments. The listserv goes automatically into an email account where you can respond to the group or individual posting the question. The difference between a listserv and any of the other services described above is that in order to participate in the conversation, you need to subscribe. Listservs can be found by searching Google or any other search engine. Many listservs are closed to the general public and only members are allowed to get the information. For example, if you are a young public relations professional and would like to get information from the Young

PR Pro listserv, search on Google for the group, click on the link and join the group. By doing so, you will gain access to the listserv which allows you to participate in conversations and post questions.

Search Engine Optimization (SEO)

A process to get your web site, blog or anything else on the Internet to appear higher up on the rankings of popular searches engines like Google and Yahoo.

SMS or Text Messages

Messages sent through your mobile telephone. They are becoming more and more popular every day. Interestingly, it started as a tool that many teenagers used to communicate with each other instead of placing a phone call. Today, adults and business owners use it to submit a quick message to another party. Oftentimes, I will get a text message from a business associate saying, "I'm running late," or "I'll be there in five minutes." Text messages are also used for marketing businesses. For example, real estate businesses have been using text messages on the lawn signs of a seller's home. If a caller dials up the number on his/her cell phone, details about the home will be displayed. Text messages are also being used for point of purchase as well. Many of the larger companies are starting to put codes on their products so that consumers can get more information on the products via text.

Social Bookmarking

A way for you to store, manage, organize and search for web

pages. There are popular places to go like Delicious where you can store articles that you read and want to save in one place. There are other social bookmarking tools like Digg and Stumbled Upon where you can actually tag something that you think is interesting and then it will be ranked, which helps increase your SEO.

Now that you have the important terms down, the next chapter demonstrates how to use social media to promote your business.

Using Social Media to Promote Your Business

3

"*In today's media landscape, it is important to be where your customers are. Kodak has always embraced this marketing philosophy and today that means being active in social media.*

The exciting thing about social media is that it offers the opportunity to engage in two-way conversation with your customers. What better way to know how to better serve your customers than to hear directly from them? Social media has enabled new ways to initiate conversations, respond to feedback and maintain an active dialogue with our customers.

Kodak has pages on Facebook (for the company and our Kodak Challenge PGA golf partnership), as well as three of our own blogs at www.kodak.com -- 1000words.kodak.com, PluggedIn. kodak.com and GrowYourBiz.kodak.com. These blogs start conversations as I mentioned before and they also have a direct positive impact on Kodak's search engine rankings.

In addition, Kodak receives more than 11,000 mentions in

other authors' blogs every month, in the form of product reviews, solicitation for opinions on products, experience with Kodak products, rants, fan mail and more. We directly participate in many of these conversations to ensure our customers know we're listening and to share answers and additional insights.

Kodak-produced podcasts, including amazing interviews with exciting young professional photographers, are available for free download at iTunes, as well as at kodak.com and YouTube. We also have several videos -- from product videos to ads to event footage -- that have been posted at YouTube (check out KodakTube at http://www.youtube.com/user/kodaktube).

The latest trend, Twitter, has become an important part of Kodak's social media activity as well. I actively twitter (@JeffreyHayzlett), as does Kodak's Chief Blogger Jenny Cisney (@KodakCB) and several of our employees. We have seen very tangible returns from our participation in Twitter, including media coverage, sales leads, increased consideration and direct product purchase."

Jeffrey W. Hayzlett, Chief Marketing Officer
Eastman Kodak Company

* * *

Building a community takes time and patience. Start by joining a few key social networking sites identified in the chapters that follow. Create a community within your sphere of influence -- your friends, your business associates and your acquaintances. Build on that foundation by looking at your friends' friends. Soon, you will have dozens of people following you and you will be following dozens of people. The more active you are on these social networking sites, the more people will want to be your friend.

Make sure when you are building your community that you qualify the people that want to get involved. Here are some important questions to ask yourself when building a community:

- Why am I building this community?
- What am I trying to promote?
- Who will use this site and what will it do for them?
- Who will build this community? (One person should spearhead the effort.)
- Will my community interact with each other?
- What if my community criticizes my product or me? (You can't control your community because each member has a voice. The more a company welcomes—even celebrates criticism—the stronger it bonds to its community.)
- What ideas and opinions will you be sharing?
- How will you market and publicize the community?

By building a community and marketing to it, you will be known as an authority on the topic because you are the founder of the community. In other words, as the founder, you are the one with the knowledge on the topic and it makes you the expert.

How Do You Get Started?

Start with one social networking site and then add a few more to make sure that you get a well-rounded audience. In the following chapters, you will find information on social networking sites available for your usage. Select the ones that are the best for your company and have the right demographics. Talk with your clients and find out what social networking site(s) they use. Log onto your target sites and get started. Fill in all the pertinent information about yourself and your business. Make sure to put in all your business information including your email address so that people can contact you. This information also adds to credibility. (You would be surprised to see how many people leave this important information out.)

In addition to joining social networking sites, you may consider setting up a blog. A blog should be about your field of expertise. On my blog (www.hilarytopper.com), I like to have relevant stories about PR and marketing, but also some life experience stories to make the blog more appealing for a general audience. Some of my blogs include posts on my travels, news stories that I have read that resonate and pertinent conversations that I have with colleagues and friends. When you only talk about one topic, it becomes limiting and your readers will get bored. Find ways to keep things interesting. It also helps people get to know you and have a dialog with you, the point of building a community. In addition, people like doing business with those they know and have similar interests.

On my social networking sites, I have a link to my blog, the HJMT website (www.hjmt.com) and the HJMT Newsroom (www.hjmtnewsroom.com). The HJMT Newsroom enables me to post news releases and microblog reporters, letting them know a new story is up with valuable resources. Then I follow up either through email or phone. I also have an RSS feed so that if they have an aggregator like Bloglines, they will receive all of my news releases in one place. I also link to my other sites, which helps my search engine optimization. Linking all of my sites together and then linking sites using keywords (words that are often searched), enables my blog to get more hits or readers. A keyword is anything that is relevant to the blog entry that you are writing. If you are writing about marketing and you use the word "marketing" many times, you may want to link "marketing" to its definition. Another example, if you are writing about the American Heart Association, you may want to link to the American Heart Association web site.

When I started my blog in March 2008, I had 400 unique visitors after a month. In May 2009, my unique visitor counter hit nearly 15,000 unique visitors each month.

Let's say you want to introduce a new product. You can invite bloggers to review the product and write about it.

Become more interactive, interesting and appealing to your community by adding a podcast or video podcast. You can record a podcast (see Chapter 24) and place it on iTunes and an RSS feed. You can record a video podcast (see Chapter 24) and place it on YouTube (see Chapter 25), MySpace TV and other video sites.

After doing this, microblog on a consistent basis. The more you microblog, the louder your message will be heard.

If you have multiple social networking sites, use either Hellotxt. com or Ping.fm. These free sites link all of your social networking sites together and allow you to post your updates in one place, changing your status line on all of your different social media sites.

Marketing to your community and engage conversations by using the different features, including discussions, photos, videos, wall postings, reviews and so on. Before you know it, you will be building an online community of followers and marketing to that community. This will entice your customers to learn more about you or the product offered. It makes a personal connection and engages your target audience and will lead to business.

Social Media Plan

No matter what type of business you have, your business will benefit from a social media plan. The plan should include the following:

- Four or five social networking sites – join as many groups as possible and gather up as many friends as you can. These sites should also include some microblogging sites, like Twitter.

- Open up an aggregator, or feed reader like Hellotxt.com or Ping.fm, that will link all of your social networking sites together so you can send out your status line or microblog to all of your sites at the same time. (A caution though, what you say to one audience will be read by all. You can't turn on and off the feed. Once it's on, it's on.)

- Develop a blog.

- Guest blog on other blog sites that relate to your field or target your particular market.

- Don't forget to include podcasts and video podcasts in your plan. Although this will be discussed later in the book, it is important to remember to link these to your blog and social networking sites.

- Make sure to keep up your social media activity. Get your message out as often as possible and be as honest and credible, by adding supporting links to other sites that are reliable sites.

Once you implement the plan, it is critical to continue to be interactive with your community. If you stop, your community will no longer follow or listen to you and your message.

Real Life Examples

One of our clients wrote a science fiction book, which was self-published. The only place it sold was on Amazon.com. They came to HJMT to get more exposure for the book. We put their book on MySpace, Facebook and some other sites. We blogged about it and we had the author guest blog about the book on science fiction related blog sites. The author received so much exposure via the Internet and viral marketing (see Chapter 28) that a book publishing company decided they wanted to publish the book!

Another real life example includes a client who wanted to introduce a new product to the market. They invented a screwdriver with an LED light embedded into the tip of the tool so that users could easily see what they are doing in dark and hard-to-reach places. As a result of a compilation of blogging, guest blogging, YouTube, microblogging and social networking sites, the product was picked up by several popular blogs, online news sites and in major newspapers across the country. Hundreds and hundreds of orders came in due to these social media tactics!

Dunkin' Donuts knows how to use social networking to build their business. They are active on Twitter and Facebook. On Twitter, they microblog about various promotions and link their microblog back to their web site. Visitors to their web site can then print out coupons, which are redeemable at any Dunkin' Donuts store. Now Dunkin' Donuts' marketing department has a way to track its ROI's (Return on Investment) by tracking the coupons and the stores in which they were used. Think about the savings they have made by using social media to get their message out. It is far less expensive than running a newspaper ad or a television commercial.

Another household brand worth mentioning is Burger King. The company has made some interesting forays into the world of online marketing. Recently they posted a notice on their Facebook account asking their friends to de-friend 10 people and as a result receive a coupon for a free Whopper. (I guess they were asking people to choose between their friends and a good burger!)

Skittles is another social marketing pioneer. In March 2009, the company launched a new interactive site. Skittles' home page was their Wikipedia page. Now, the home page is their Twitter page. You can also quickly link to their YouTube videos, photos in Flickr (a social networking site that primarily stores and shares photos and videos) (see Chapter 10) and Facebook page. When on the Skittles web site, visitors click on the header "media" are taken to their YouTube or Flickr page. When visitors click on the header "friends," they are taken to the company's Facebook page. Skittles uses its social media sites to make up its new web site. It no longer has a traditional site. It just uses its social networking sites to get its message out!

Other companies use YouTube videos to build awareness and recognition for their product or service. YouTube videos get consumers involved in the brand and builds brand advocates. For example, Blendtec (a blending appliance company), has a series of online commercials called, "Will it Blend?" The CEO takes regular objects like a rake, a Rubik's cube, marbles and even an iPhone and puts it into his blender and makes it blend. According to management, these YouTube video helped increase sales for the blender by 700%!

Recently I visited Great Wolf Lodge in Pennsylvania, a Pocono's resort with a huge indoor water park. I sat in the hotel room, surfing the Internet and came across Great Wolf's community on YouTube. It encouraged guests and past guests to post videos on the site of the fun they had at the water park. I viewed a few of the videos and forwarded them to friends who I thought would be interested in the place. I also blogged about Great Wolf Lodge and microblogged about it. Everyone posting information on the web helped create viral marketing for the resort. As a result of my blog, my niece went on a trip to Great Wolf Lodge. Even better, Great Wolf is getting its paying customers to do its marketing for them!

Using Blogs and Microblogs

"It's important to direct people you connect with using Social Networking back to your Blog. Blogs create an expert and authority status and brand you as well as your business."

Gina Sprenkle, President
http://GinaSprenkle.com

* * *

Maybe you've heard a lot about blogs and blogging but don't really know what they are and what they are used for. A blog is a weblog or online diary. It can help you build a presence in a crowded marketplace. It's written in an informal manner as if you were speaking with someone. It can delve into topics about travel, media, parenthood, weight loss, fitness and so much more!

I started my blog in March 2008. I have hundreds of posts about everything from current clients, to annoying situations, to family matters, staffing issues and running a small business. When my blog was nominated as a finalist in the 2008 Stevie

Awards for Women in Business as the Blog of the Year, it helped me gain recognition from industry leaders, some of who are now clients. Recently, I started accepting guest bloggers to make the site more interesting and appealing to a wide range of people.

Why Blog?

My husband thinks it is crazy to let people know so much information about you. By blogging, he believes, you are putting yourself in jeopardy and undermining your security. Perhaps he has a point. Therefore, I am mindful about my blog and what information I make available. More than 15,000 unique visitors a month read my blog. These unique visitors are potential customers who may want to know something about me. They want to relate to me as a person first and an expert second. Through my blog, I want to let these potential customers know that I am an honest businesswoman with a lot of integrity. They are able to see me in a different light, in a more personal way and establish a deeper connection. As we all know, people do business with people they like. My blog is the first step to getting to know the type of person I am and the way I run my business. Hopefully, they like me and will want to learn more about ways in which my staff and I can help them! The blog also increases the Search Engine Optimization (SEO) for my company's web site.

Increasing Your SEO

Besides utilizing my blog to link back to my company web site, I also help increase the SEO for my actual blog by linking to things that I talk about in my blog entries. For example, if I talk about Enterprise Rent-A-Car, I will link their name to their corporate web site. Every time I mention a company name, I link to their web site. In addition, you can "tag" several different key words as well. These words are used as Meta tags (HTML tag that often appears on the top of your web site) and every time they come up on the Internet they will link to other places that it appears.

I recently installed Zemanta (a free downloadable program) on my blog. When I open my blog, Zemanta opens automatically with a variety of photos to choose from and various links to other blogs. This enables me to link to relevant photos that appear on Flickr and other stories that appear on other blogs that are related to what I am talking about. This also helps my SEO because it tags and links my site to various other sites.

Where to Blog

So you want to blog, but don't know how to do it? There are several different services on the web that are free to use, including the two most popular services, Wordpress and Blogger.com. Blogger.com (blogspot.com) is much easier to set up than Wordpress. You can establish a blog in less than 10 minutes. However, Wordpress enables you to do more with the blog to include pluggins and advanced customized tools. Most media outlets use Wordpress so that they could easily update and change the customization of the blog. The other major difference is with content and ownership rights. According to the blog site, "Search for Blogging," it states that since Google owns Blogger.com, they own your content. On the other hand, you own your own content with Wordpress. Many designers work with Wordpress and can easily set you up with a customized blog for a nominal design fee.

Your First Post

So, you've decided that blogging is for you. You visit Wordpress or Blogger.com and open up a blog. Now what's next? What do you write about?

The first post should be an introduction as to who you are and why you're writing. Also, give your readers an overview of what the blog will be about. After that, make sure to blog often. Don't blog once and not blog again for a week or two or even three. I know some folks who have blogs and have not updated them in months. The more you update, the more people will follow your posts. If you don't update your blog on a regular basis, then readers will lose interest and the few times you do post will be a waste of time.

Pick a Theme

Blog about a specific topic. For example some people blog about business related issues, like Seth Godin, author of *Tribes* and *Purple Cow*. Others write about new social media/networking topics like Mashable – The Social Media Guide and Chris Bogan, community and social media expert. While others blog about travels, skiing, parenting or even being a small business owner.

How Will People Find You?

People will find you through Wordpress or Blogger.com. They will also find you through search engines with key words. For example, if someone is looking for a recommendation on a hotel in Cancun and your blog focuses on travel, your blog will come up in the search engine result page.

In addition, consider marketing your blog. Tell everyone you have a blog. Make sure that they know when there is a new post and new information to keep the blog timely.

When I have a new post, I microblog and send a link to my online community via my social network. I also include my blog in my signature line in all of my emails. By doing this, I pick up new readers with every entry.

Blog Comments

Are you able to monitor comments? Of course. On Wordpress and Blogger.com you will receive an email that enables you to see and approve each new blog comment. If you would like to reject the comment because it may be offensive or irrelevant, you can do so here and the comment will never make it to the post. If you accept the comment, then it will appear with the post for life.

Typepad (a free program that manages your blog site) offers an application that enables your blog to become more interactive. It allows members of your community to talk with each other and converse on your blog. Instead of just a one sided conversation, you can now have informative discussions about various topics in your blog.

Microblogging

Microblogging is a short blog post that you can use to promote an idea, product or service. This is more commonly known as status updating. You only have 140 characters to get your message out. On each posting, you can promote your blog.

Here are some microblogs that I recently posted:

- Looking for bloggers to review a new cookie. Visit www.gsnc.org
- New Art in the White House? Check out www.hilarytopper.com
- I'm using http://zemanta.com, a really cool blogger's assistant. Try it and share your thoughts #zemanta
- What rental car do you use? Visit erac.com

When using Twitter or any other microblogging tool, make sure to check your replies and your direct responses. You will be surprised how many people will answer your questions or even link to your blog!

Be sure to microblog about occurrences in your organization at least five times a day. Remember to be conversational (hence, conversational media) in tone and post things that people will find interesting. Also, don't be shy about getting involved in dialogs with those who reach out to you in response to your postings. The more discussions you have with your community, the more people will be engaged.

Using Blogs to Promote Your Product or Service

In addition to having your own blog, you may consider either guest blogging on another site or having bloggers write about your product or service.

Many restaurants use bloggers to write restaurant reviews for them. They contact the bloggers, offer them a "free dinner" in exchange for a write-up and the bloggers post about the restaurant, service and food. These bloggers post their reviews and then share with their own community. For example, if you have 10 bloggers writing about your restaurant and they have a community of at least 100 people each, more than 1,000 people will read about your restaurant. Then those 1,000 people share the blog with their friends and now 2,000 people will learn about you.

Other businesses use bloggers to review their products and services as well. Authors, new product introductions, services and even dental offices work with bloggers to promote their business.

Pay-per-blog is a relatively new service where consumers are actually paid a minimal amount to write about a subject matter. If you are a coffee manufacturer, for example and want people to review the coffee, you may go on the pay-per-blog site and ask people to write about your product or service. By clicking on pay-per-blog in a Google search, you will find numerous sites that will actually pay you to post a blog. (You can't get rich here, but it could add a little extra cash in your wallet.)

Years ago, the power belonged in the hands of the media. Today, it's the bloggers that influence what we eat, what we drink, where we go for fun and what we do on a Saturday evening.

Blogging is the ultimate word of mouth marketing technique. One recommendation leads to another and before you know it, dozens, hundreds, thousands or even millions of people hear about something all through viral marketing. But remember, when you blog, be honest and authentic!

Transparency is key! Don't always blog about the same thing either. Variety is a necessity! Whenever I blog about personal stuff, I get many more responses than when I blog about business. However, I know that people do read the business content because they always mention something about a past blog post when I see them or they write about it on a social networking site.

Viewing Your Stats

On every blogging application, you have the ability to monitor or track how many people are looking at your blog. Many of these programs will enable you to see which post was most popular and which was least popular. On Blogger.com, you can install a counter to see how many people have visited your site. Counters are free and can come from Google Analytics, FreeStats, Easy Hit Counter or StatCounter.

On Wordpress.com, a free stat counter is included in the site. To install it, use your Wordpress.com API key (sent to you when you sign up). Once the counter is installed it begins running and collecting information about the blogger's page views, the most popular posts and pages, where blog traffic is coming from and what people click on when they leave. It also adds a link to your dashboard so you can see your blog's stats on one page.

Adding Pings

Once you publish your blog post, you can ping it through pingomatic.com. This web site will take your blog and help to make it more mainstream by attaching it to various sites like Bloglines (an aggregator that puts all your blogs in one place), Yahoo, Technorati (allows you to search in real time for blogs by tags or keywords) and so on. Another tool, Feedburner (a free program that allows bloggers and podcasters the ability to manage their RSS feeds and track usage of their subscribers) also increases traffic to your blog site.

Social Networking Sites

"Our primary focus on using "social media" tools is to form a more personal connection with our employees and customers.

If you're trying to use these tools to sell, you're already off the mark."

Tony Hsieh, CEO
Zappos.com

* * *

What are Social Networking Sites?

Social networking sites are places on the Internet where people can interact directly with each other.

According to Wikipedia:

"Social networking sites focus on building online communities of people who share common interests and/or activities or who are interested in exploring the interests and activities of others. Most social networking sites are web based and provide a variety of ways for users to interact, such as e-mail and instant messaging services.

Social networking has created new ways to communicate and share information. Social networking websites are being used regularly by millions of people and it now seems that social networking will be an enduring part of everyday life. The main types of social networking services are those, which contain directories of some categories (such as former classmates), means to connect with friends (usually with self-description pages) and recommender systems linked to trust."

Once you start social networking, there will be sites you favor and frequent often. Lately, I've been using Plaxo, Facebook, LinkedIn, FriendFeed, Twitter, Yammer, Flickr and Seesmic. Although these may be right for me at the moment, after reading this book, you will determine which social networking sites are right for you.

There are hundreds of social networking sites on the Internet. Most people know about the popular ones such as Facebook, Twitter and MySpace, but there are so many more out there, including Bebo (see Chapter 7), Plurk (see Chapter 18) and even Koornk (see Chapter 15). Each country has dozens of its own social networking sites as well. There are also social networking sites for individualized interests.

Everyday, another social networking site appears on the Internet. I recently discovered Millionheads.com, which is a social networking site that allows people to ask questions. People around the world have the ability to answer your questions and at the end, you get a pie chart that tells you what the audience response is to your question.

I was on the site a few weeks ago and one of the questions was -- should I buy brown boots or black boots? The majority of the respondents said black boots. When you have a tough pressing question for which you would like anonymous answers, go to Millionheads.com and just ask.

LoudHive.com is another site I recently discovered. It enables you to position yourself as a subject expert. When registering for the site, you need to specify areas of expertise. Visitors type in questions and an expert on LoudHive.com answers. If someone has a question in your area of expertise, you will be notified and given the chance to impart your knowledge.

Lastly, I became hooked to Seesmic, an online video community. Like Facebook, you get to follow friends. Unlike Facebook, you can ask questions to the entire Seesmic community by recording a short video. People then answer with their own video responses! It's a dynamic site and definitely worth a look!

Many business publications, including *Businessweek* and *Inc.* magazine, have social networking sites. I've even noticed some business writers coming up with new social networking communities like Seth Godin's *Tribes*. The Girl Scouts recently formed their own social networking community and other new ones form every day.

You can easily develop your own social networking site on a free Internet program called ning.com (an online program that enables you to create your own community).

Why Use Social Networking Sites?

Social networking sites enable people to get to know each other better. There are only so many hours in a day and so many days in a week and everyone has a very busy lifestyle. Social networking helps people connect with one another more effectively and on a more personal level than any other forum.

For example, I have friends on Facebook that I could never connect with outside of an online community. This is a common occurrence among Facebook users. It's also a great tool to reconnect with people who you haven't seen in years. I have two childhood friends with whom I recently reconnected with on Facebook and we have actually crossed over from the virtual world to the real world by meeting in person.

Sometimes, you will find many people in the virtual world want to stay there. They don't want to cross over and I find that fascinating. They want to talk with you on Facebook, but when you suggest getting together for coffee, they don't want to do it. Everyone has their reasons for being on these social networking sites. My reason is to strengthen my connections and build business for my public relations firm. Simply chatting online may just satisfy others.

Through social networking sites, I have gotten to know numerous people that I would otherwise not have had the chance to meet. I have also launched networking groups online and have met a lot of people through this group. Now, I have the opportunity to learn about people from their social networking sites. I can see what we have in common, our interests, hobbies or family and then when I do finally get together with them, we have something to talk about - we have an established connection.

One key to using social networking sites to develop business is to first create a community with others online. Evaluate the sites and figure out which ones work for you. Perhaps four or five of them are beneficial and the rest are not relevant to your niche market. Or, you may want to be on as many social networking sites as possible. The key is to gather contacts together and create a community that will enable you to interact, get feedback and learn what your consumers like and dislike.

Remember, each social networking site targets a different audience; however, most sites do share a lot of common ground. As a matter of fact, most social networking sites are more similar then they are different.

In subsequent chapters, we will explore various social networking sites. In this hands-on guide, you will be able to review each site and decide which sites work best for your business.

Do You Know
Where Your Friends Are?
-Brightkite.com

*"I use Brightkite for posting pictures of restaurants
I frequent and travel that I do. My immediate
family is on Brightkite and it makes it easy to have
everyone know what you are up to all the time,"*

Jack Mahrt
Campbell, CA

*   *   *

If you want people to know where you are at every moment of
the day, Brightkite is for you. In real time, you will see where
your friends and others are in your network. If your privacy
setting is not on, you will see people all around the world and
their locations. This is a great site for a huge sales staff to see
where everyone in a company is at every moment. It's also a

good new business development tool because you can research business people who work around your current location.

Brightkite has an eclectic mix of people on the site. You can find contacts through both Facebook and Twitter by downloading the appropriate applications. Brightkite encourages users to input their frequented locations. Once at a defined location, you can view others in similar locations. All of the site's functionality is also available with the iPhone web application.

Signing Up

Anyone can sign up for Brightkite. The first step is to create a username and password.

The username will be available to those who follow you. (I like to use the same username on all of my social networking sites for branding purposes.)

Personalizing Your Profile

A profile reveals likes and dislikes and enables people to learn more about you. You can include your company information, its mission, your web site and any other content you wish to share. In addition, you have an opportunity to upload your photo allowing others to put a face to a name and helping to portray a particular image – professional, artistic and so on.

Features on Brightkite

Brightkite has a lot of features, including:

Public/Private

You will have the option to make the account public or private.

If you have a public account, you can meet new people, search activities in the area and find new hot spots. A private account can control who views your account and at what level of detail. The only drawback with a private account is that it limits the number of people you can meet.

Check In Now

Checking in can let your friends know your location. Every time you check in from a different location, it reconfigures the list of people near you. This feature is great for companies in which most of the employees are on the road. This enables the employer to keep track of their employee's current locations all in one spot! In addition, it enables salespeople to discover and meet new prospects in selected locations.

What's Happening

Below is a list of pages within the what's happening page:

- **Me and My Friends** Tells what you and your Brightkite friends are doing, including – updates on check-ins, status updates and wall posts.

- **Around Me** Lists what other people are doing. These people are not always members of your friend network. (Depending on your privacy setting, you will appear on others sites as well.)

- **Mentions** Tells when people include you in their post(s).

- **Comments** List when people comment on your post(s).
- **Universe** Shows what is happening to people in all locations, not just in your area.

Friends

You can search for friends through your address book, from your Gmail account or followers on Twitter. You can also email friends to sign up.

Placemarks

Placemarks allow you to name your locations. If, for example, you sign in and input your location as Babylon, NY, you can then rename this location as home. You can also name your office address as office or work.

Visited Places

This is a map that lets you see all the places you visited upon signing into your account.

People Near Me

This is a listing of all of the people signed in within 4,000 meters of your location/placemark. When you check in from a different location, the list of people near you changes.

Links

Your account can be linked with Facebook, Flickr, Last.fm (billed as the world's largest online music catalogue), LinkedIn, MySpace and Twitter. This means that status lines, photos and other information posted on this site will appear on those other sites and vice versa!

Wall

You can enable the wall or message board in your profile. The wall allows you and your friends to communicate directly.

David Parmet, a friend and social media guru, uses Brightkite. One day he was in a museum in Chicago. He found out that a friend of his, whom he hadn't seen in a long time, was in the same museum on the floor below. Thanks to Brightkite, they were able to connect. Brightkite, he says, is a great tool to find out the locations of friends and business associates.

MY 2 CENTS

I like that Brightkite is different than most other social media sites. It doesn't get the publicity enjoyed by Facebook or Twitter, but it does serve a valuable purpose when used for business. If you are a business development officer or salesperson, Brightkite is a good tool to find prospects, clients and colleagues in locations around you. For example, there may be a prospect you have been targeting for your business who is within blocks of your current position. It may make sense for you to reach out to that person to connect.

Bebo is Under-Rated...
-Bebo.com

"I use Bebo to make business contacts, find affiliates for my business www.sweetwatergardensngifts.com and connect with old schoolmates and family and friends. It has increased my business tremendously and been a blessing personally as well."

Dana Rankin
Kansas City, MO
http://www.sweetwatergardensngifts.com/
http://therecipediva.wordpress.com

* * *

Bebo has a fresh new look compared to some of the other social networking sites out there. Its homepage, allows you to have a to-do list; link with your AOL, Yahoo mail or Gmail accounts so that you conveniently have all your mail in one place. Application recommendations are on the right-hand side of the page where you can install anything from "Which Sponge Bob character are you like?" to "What song are you?"

The home page also includes all of your microblog feeds from Twitter, Flickr and Hellotxt.com.

Like other social networking sites, Bebo's homepage allows you to inform people in the network about yourself, music you like and your relationship/marital status. There is a wall, comment area, quiz area and polls. You can even have a Bebo blog.

When an account is created, the profile is private by default, this limits access to friends you specifically add. You can select the "Public Profile" option so the profile will still be visible to any other members of a group who may have joined.

One of Bebo's more interesting features is the open media platform, which allows companies to distribute content to the Bebo community. Content providers can import their media player (allows you to download music and video) to Bebo and monetize the advertising within it. Each content provider has a specialized page designed for video, which showcases any Adobe Flash video content at the top of the profile. Many of the major media outlets are signed up for the service, including CBS, Sky, Ustream.tv, BBC and Last.fm. They do this to build their audience and their brand.

Major Companies are Using Bebo

Major companies like NIKE, Dunkin' Donuts and Ed Hardy that market to entertainers, musicians, artists, etc. have profiles on Bebo. The lessons we can learn from these companies are that Facebook and Twitter are not the only viable social networking sites. There are others that are just as valuable to specific markets.

Signing Up

Complete the sign up application, which requires your name, gender, date of birth (you can opt to hide your age!), email address, password for logging into the site and a security check (they provide a word and you type it into a provided box). This is done so that spammers can't access the site.

The site will then ask you if you would like to check for your friends or contacts on Bebo. They will ask for your email or IM name and password. You can skip this step if you choose to do so.

Features on Bebo

Some of the features on Bebo include:

- Search popular web sites
- View popular videos
- Find popular music artists
- Find popular music videos
- Find popular authors
- Find popular books
- Create/Join interest groups

Bebo seems to be is geared for the more artistic audience – musicians, artists, entertainers, etc. Groups are not focused on business but rather on the arts. The other interesting feature is that you can change your profile page to have any skin that you want. I was able to change my skin several times and was able to give my profile completely different looks. Now, I have pink hearts on my profile. The reason why you may want to change your look is to keep your audience engaged. What will he/she think of next?

Add Life Streams to Your Changes Feed

Here you can add your Flickr and Twitter links for Bebo members to follow you.

Requests Made

This section keeps track of those you have requested as friends as well as those who have requested the same of you.

Write Stories

In this section, you can write stories about how you met certain people.

Skins

These are images that are created by Bebo users through photoshop or art editing programs that can be placed in email messages or on profiles. Search for skins through the Bebo database or create your own by clicking on the roll your own icon and following the step-by-step instructions.

Music

This section allows you to find information about the music

industry. Here, you can also upload your unsigned band (if you have one!) to Bebo by clicking on the sign up link and following the step-by-step instructions.

Groups

Bebo has hundreds of groups that you can join in order to increase the amount of friends you have. Add groups to your profile that are of interest to you or your company.

I've also noticed that a lot of agents and others selling to this market also have sites on Bebo. If music, entertainment or the arts is your market, this site is for you.

MY 2 CENTS

Bebo has thousands of users in the entertainment industry. This is a perfect site for anyone who is targeting that industry. It works similar to Facebook and other social networking sites and has a nice clean, very professional look. It links all of your status lines or microblogs to the status line on Bebo and tells you who has looked at your site. This gives you an idea of interest. For business, consider targeting those looking at your site on Bebo. I also like the fan pages and the links to new music groups. Bebo is indeed under-rated and most definitely worth a look.

Is it all About Business Exchange? -Bx.Businessweek.com

"BusinessWeek Exchange is one of the most inventive, creative ideas to come along in a long time. It takes the idea of user in user-generated content and does something really interesting with it. It brings companies into the fold as users – presenting a unique and potentially controversial way of looking at contributed content. I believe we won't see the full impact of what BusinessWeek Exchange – and others to come – will have for at least the next year and probably the next 2 to 3 years. I factor blog networks from Fast Company, Wired and the like into this, too. They're allowing CEOs (and other, usually C-level company people) to contribute to the dialogue as though they're reporters under the

guise of a blog. Again, authority and influence changes with the title of the person writing. That is, when and if the user – meaning reader – realizes it, which they inevitably will."

Jennifer Lindsay, Director of Digital Services,
Social Media Evangelist/New Media Guru
Eastwick Communications

*   *   *

BusinessWeek magazine has the right approach. Since they know the value of social networking, they created Business Exchange where business people can connect with one another. Interestingly, when logging into Business Exchange, visitors can also view the top news stories on *BusinessWeek*, the magazine. You can save news stories to your home page along with interesting relevant news articles. This makes the site quite useful and helps *BusinessWeek* build a loyal following.

Business Exchange is arranged by topics. Topics are sorted by functional areas such as Business Law, Small Business Marketing and Search Engine Optimization. There are also more specific or timely areas such as the fall of Lehman Brothers, the Federal Reserve bailout of Bear Stearns and even the latest business strategies of Starbucks.

Business Exchange lets you bookmark business news, blog articles, tools and additional online resources to share with others. You can bookmark just about any format of online content including videos, tools and white papers. Readers can also comment on news items submitted.

Upon registering Business Exchange you set up a profile. Those who belong to the social networking site, LinkedIn, can import their LinkedIn profile sparing duplicate efforts of filling out yet another profile.

MY 2 CENTS

I like that this site suggests people that I may want to include in my network. Through this feature, I actually met a business owner in India, with whom I regularly correspond. My connections are networked to people who post interesting articles attached to their sites. Business Exchange also has links to Twitter, which is very helpful, especially when I seek to connect with reporters or business development people to grow my business. I like that the site offers news feeds to interesting articles and blog sites that prompt lively conversations. You can also post an article or a blog entry as well. There are only business people on this site and it is relatively easy to network with people who you may not otherwise meet. The only problem I see with the site is that it doesn't have many active participants. It would benefit the site to promote to business owners on Facebook, Plaxo, LinkedIn and Twitter.

W'sup Facebook!
-Facebook.com

"Facebook has shown me how we have such an intertwined social network. It is interesting to see who knows whom. It is more like 3 degrees of separation!"

Erica Garay, Partner
Meyer, Suozzi, English & Klein, PC

"I mainly use Facebook and it's been a nice way to reconnect with old friends and keep up with family and business acquaintances. I've only used it to reach out to potential story sources a few times, though I must admit, it worked. I worry about privacy issues, however and am increasingly careful who I "friend." I also have some concern about the irreversibility of items posted in haste coming back to haunt folks."

Marcelle Fischler, Writer/Editor

*　　*　　*

More than two years ago, my 10-year-old son put me on Facebook as a joke. He thought it would be funny and he wanted to tease his older sister by having mom on the site trying to spy on her. The joke turned into the best thing that ever happened! My first friend was reporter, Marcelle Fischler of the *New York Times* and then reporter, Jamie Herzlick from *Newsday* and the list goes on.

As I got more and more into Facebook, I discovered that I could create groups and invite my friends to different events that I was promoting. I also learned that I could keep up with past employees, learn about my future employees and even get a deeper understanding of my clients.

Why is Facebook so popular? It allows you to share interests and post news on both a personal and business level.

Facebook is a social networking web site where you can join networks organized by region, city, workplace, school, families, product, venue or cause, connect and interact with other people. There are more than 55,000 regional, work-related, collegiate and high school networks. The site has more than 175 million active users (and growing everyday) and the fastest growing demographic are those 35 years of age and older.

Connecting on Facebook

Former Employees

It's important to keep up with former employees, especially those who ended on good terms. (You never know if they will become future clients or even employees again!) I keep up with several of my former employees. They were very dedicated and I am genuinely interested in what they are doing. Other benefits to keeping up with former employees include potential referral sources and you can share information like future networking events.

Future Employees

Facebook is a great way to check out someone's background. You get an opportunity to view photos, check out their friends and even get a sense of their interests. This enables me to find out if these potential employees are a good fit with my current staff.

When I was at a business lunch the other day, an attorney friend told me that he only hires staff with whom he would have lunch with. Facebook allows you to see what your potential employees interests are, however, if they keep their profile private, then you won't be able to access anything and that may signify a red flag.

Deeper Understanding of Clients

People want to do business with people they like. That is a fact. The more you know about your clients the more you can share common ground and cultivate a relationship that goes deeper than just business services.

Facebook enables members to learn about compelling aspects of people's lives. Participants frequently update their status line. Some people use it to tell what they are doing while others post about a situation, a problem, a call for resources, a link to their blog or an informative post.

Developing New Relationships with Potential Clients

Another way to use Facebook is to develop new relationships with potential clients. Here you find out their interests and details about their families. It gives you an opportunity to make a connection with them on another level and build lasting bonds. Social media is all about relationship building and Facebook allows you to do just that.

My established clients have invited me to be their Facebook friends. And I have met potential clients on Facebook because I am very active. I consistently update my status. I also join groups and comment on the status of others by offering advice, congratulating them on the news they post or sharing an upbeat sentiment.

Personalizing Your Profile

Your profile is the place to list your likes, dislikes, music preferences and favorite movies. It is where you describe how you earn your living, past positions, the schools you attended and more. There is the opportunity to post a great deal of information in this section and you should try to utilize it. Through your profile, people will get to know you better and the more people know you, the more people will relate to you and want to do business with you.

The Profile Photo

On Facebook, as on many of the other social networking sites, you have an opportunity to post either a photo of yourself or an avatar (a character or an image). What does this photo say about you? I like to use a professional photo because I don't know who views my site. But, I know other professionals who use Disney figures or make funny faces as their photo. This shows that they are not buttoned up. They are creative and independent. While it is okay to use family or personal photos, be careful not to use a photo that you may not want everyone to see including a potential client or employer.

Privacy Settings

Many people ask me if there is a privacy setting on Facebook and the answer is yes. There are different levels of privacy. You can permit the entire Facebook community to see your information, allow limited information or make your Facebook page private so that no one sees it unless they are friends. I recommend to keep the profile public if you are using Facebook for business development. This way more people will see your information.

Features on Facebook

To understand the power of Facebook, learn about its various elements. Listed below are some of the basic foundations:

Your Wall

For those of you who have never used a social networking site, the wall is a new phenomenon. The wall features a status line, where your friends can leave comments. (For more on status lines see Chapter 4 on microblogging.) Your friends can also comment on your wall. They can even ask you questions and carry on a conversation. If there is one thing to remember, it's this: **the wall is not a private conversation!** Other Facebook members can see what you write on your wall.

For example, in a post I made as a joke to a friend, I wrote that I took a photograph while driving and ended the post by saying "but don't tell anyone!" This spurred a lot of conversation, including a friend who is a police officer telling me to pull over!

Finding Friends

To grow your community, start by using the search feature (located on the upper right hand top corner of the page). Enter your high school and put in your graduating year. You will be surprised how many people who graduated with you are on Facebook! I've found people who I was never a friend with in high school and now we are friends on Facebook. Also, search for the year you graduated college, places where you worked, current employment and then once you have five to 10 friends, look at their Facebook friends who appear on their home page. More than likely, you will find many people you know! Currently, I have nearly 1,000 friends on Facebook and my portfolio grows daily.

Photo Albums

The photo album is a great vehicle to promote past and current events, product launches and even internal meetings. Photos can be easily uploaded on Facebook and whenever you add new images the news feed posts updates on your wall for all of your friends to see. Some of the privacy settings limit what people can see.

Events

Through the Facebook event feature you can get exposure and visibility for your social or business gatherings. Many people use it for business networking groups while others use it for fundraisers. These events help you keep your community interested in what you are doing. And while it is tempting to invite everyone you know it is important to target only those who would be interested in receiving these notifications. Otherwise, your Facebook friends may see you as a nuisance and dismiss your future updates and invitations.

Groups/Fan Pages

At HJMT, we advise all of our clients to either create a group or fan page depending on their business. In addition, we recommend that they consider joining some of the numerous groups, which include: golf, music, animals, business, social media, journalism and more. There are an array of groups ranging from those for people who love skiing to those for people who have children with disabilities. They are all on Facebook. This is another vehicle from which to target a niche community, especially if you have a product or service that suits their needs.

Video

In subsequent chapters, I will cover YouTube (see Chapter 25) and other video sites, but Facebook also has the capability to upload videos. Videos can serve as great marketing tools. For example, one of my friends has a business fighting traffic tickets. He made an amusing video of a police officer pulling someone over. When the man behind the wheel opened the car door, the police officer was knocked out. He got out of the car, kicked the police officer, saw that he was down for a while and drove away. The video was staged and was uploaded to promote my friend's traffic ticket business (check out www. nyctrafficticket.com).

I also post videos on my site using my new Flip video camera. The quality of the image is good and there is even an HD version. The video is very homegrown, but that is the appeal. It's authentic and organic and that's what people on the Internet like to see.

Status

Most social networking sites have a status line. This line tells your community what you are currently doing. I like to use the status line to spread the word about my blog entries, events that we are promoting and even publicity opportunities or new product introductions. Throughout the day, I update my status so that my community sees what I am up to.

Tips for Good Status Updates

Remember to keep your status updates upbeat, not too personal, not desperate and not too revealing. You want the status to leave people with a positive impression of you.

Mobile Phone

I like mobile integration. Many sites offer this feature, but Facebook makes mobile integration particularly easy. Every time you get a new message, you see it immediately on your Blackberry or iPhone.

Facebook Marketplace

Facebook enables you and your company to advertise. Advertisers get tens of thousands of hits a day. However, each hit means the advertiser must ante up a fee to Facebook. This could be very costly, especially when people are randomly clicking a link and have no interest in the company's product or service.

The other day, I was conducting research for a dentist who recently purchased a massive amount of equipment for his office. He was considering promoting his services through online sources. I noticed that one of his competitors was on Facebook, so I clicked on the link and snooped around. Interestingly, this competitor's ad campaign had a relatively long run, which suggested that his advertising dollars worked on Facebook.

Applications

Applications on Facebook are great when they are useful and many are. However, many of the applications are silly and I basically ignore them. Some of the ones I ignore include: snowball throwing, martini drinks and giving a kiss. I just think it's a bit inappropriate for a business setting. However, these applications were not developed for people who use Facebook for business purposes. Many of the Facebook users are spillovers from when Facebook was used on college campuses.

Poking

The first time I got poked, I got annoyed. Then I realized that when someone pokes you it means that they are thinking about you. You have the option to either poke back or ignore. One of my oldest friends with whom I haven't spoken with in at least 10 years found me on Facebook. She now lives in New Jersey and every day I get a poke. It's nice because it sends me a reminder that she is now part of my community. However, you may want to save the pokes for those you know socially. Your clients and prospects may not react to pokes favorably.

MY 2 CENTS

Of all the social media sites I am on, I like the interaction and the conversation starters from Facebook best. I always seem to get a dialog going with someone I value. Facebook has helped increase visitors to my blog. I've used Facebook for the last two years and have seen substantial growth and development. As a result of my Facebook activity, I have also seen a significant increase in business.

Fotos that Flickr
–Flickr.com

"I use Flickr and Long Island Business News *uses Flickr on our website. We also have the photos stream up to our Facebook page. It has been a great tool, it's another viral way to further deepen your company's brand, to share information and share pictures in a fun and easy way, its just plain ole great marketing exposure. Flickr is an easy application to use, a nominal annual fee for unlimited storage with the ability to set your own copyrights if you desire."*

Kathleen Gobos, Associate Publisher
Long Island Business News

* * *

One of the earliest web 2.0 sites, Flickr is an image and video hosting site, web services suite and online community platform. Flickr is one of the social networking sites that I use often. I link to many of my other social networking sites through Flickr.

In addition to being a popular web site for users to share personal photographs, the service is widely used by bloggers as a photo repository. Once a photo is up on Flickr, it is up for grabs. Its popularity has been fueled by its organizational tools, which allow photos to be tagged and browsed. I use Flickr photos often when I'm blogging about a particular topic and need photos to liven up my posts. Many of the photos also appear on Google images as well.

Signing Up

To sign up for Flickr, you need a Yahoo account. I didn't have a Yahoo account, but the system makes sign up quick and easy.

To sign up, Yahoo requires a first and last name, gender, birthday, location and zip code. It then prompts registrants to select a Yahoo ID and email as well as a password. Once this is complete, registrants must verify their account, which will then direct them to the Flickr web site. There, registrants must create a Flickr nickname and create their profile. Try to use the same username throughout your social networking sites for branding and consistency purposes.

Personalizing Your Profile

Create Your Buddy Icon

Your buddy icon is a small image that appears on Flickr to represent you. Use an uploaded image or find a new image online to make your buddy icon.

Choose Your URL

Follow the prompts and share your photostream easily with friends by customizing your Flickr URL. Once created, your Flickr URL cannot be changed.

Upload Photos

Uploading photos is a simple, user-friendly process. Just make sure that the files you want to share are less than to 5 megabytes in size. Also add tags to your photos. Choose a privacy setting. The private setting allows only you, friends and/or family to see your photos. This is an invitation only area. The public setting allows everyone on Flickr to see photos. Choose an advanced setting for your uploads. Next, select the safety level (safe, moderate or restricted) and content type (photos, screenshots, art, illustrations or other non-photographic images).

Find Friends on Flickr

Find your friends on Flickr using an existing address from the following email providers:

- Yahoo Mail
- Gmail
- Windows Live Hotmail

Or, search for friends through a Flickr search.

Since I opened a Yahoo account just for Flickr, I don't have any friends on the site because I don't use the email address. I am not using this site for community building, although some people do use it for this purpose. When I use Flickr, I microblog about the posting and link my community back to my Flickr home page.

Homepage

The homepage is your main page view including:

- **Your Photostream** - View quickly your photostream.
- **Your Contacts** - See new uploads from your contacts. Use this feature also to search for new friends.
- **Explore/The Commons** - See quick view of interesting photos, popular tags and archives of the world's public photography.

Use one of the uploading tools to access a batch of photos or send your photos or video by email, which is especially helpful when uploading photos from camera phones.

Features on Flickr

Flickr is a social networking site and has a lot of features similar to other social networking sites, including:

- Sharing videos and photos
- Uploading photos
- Editing Photos
- Mapping application, showing where a photo was taken
- Organizing photos
- Tagging friends and family
- Making photo books, picture frames and DVDs

Organize

Upload photos and use the photo organization tools provided to make searching and viewing photos easier. Useful tools include: sets, collections and archives.

Sets

Organize your photos into sets, which allow you to arrange your photos into groupings based on topic.

Tags

Tags are keywords or labels that you add to a photo to make it easier to find later. Photos can be tagged with phrases or words. When looking for particular pictures click the appropriate tag and access all photos that have been categorized that way.

You may also add tags to friends' photos, if they set that option in their privacy settings.

Archives

Store photos in your archives. Organize them by the date the picture was taken or by the date posted to Flickr. When organizing photos by the date they were posted to Flickr, you can make the order of the items in your photostream more preferable.

Favorites

Collect photos and videos you like from other members and tag them as favorites.

Popular

Reveals your most popular photos based on the number of views or favorites. Friends can also comment on your most popular photos.

Profile

Go back to your profile after you've uploaded photos to change your profile picture.

Contacts

Share photos or videos with people you know in your social network. Use the contacts feature to stay in touch with photographers you like, people who share your interests or your friends and family.

From Your Friends

View new photos from your friends as soon as they arrive on Flickr. Leave comments and notes too.

Connect with People

Interact with others whenever you see a buddy icon (follow the simple prompts through the menu). Mark people as contacts, skip over to their photostream or visit their profile to learn more about them.

Groups

Share content and conversation, either privately or publicly through the group feature. Search for groups that interest you and join them. Or start your own group.

MY 2 CENTS

Flickr is a great social networking site if you have a lot of photos to post and share with your community. I use Flickr for HJMT events. After the events, I post photos and send them to the client. I also send them to prospects so that they can see what happened at one of our events. It's rewarding when prospects call me to tell me that they saw my photos on Flickr. These calls have helped me strengthen relationships and even plant seeds for opening new accounts.

All Your Friends on FriendFeed? -FriendFeed.com

"I like to pull my blogs, bookmarks, videos and images in to FriendFeed, then I can hand out the RSS feed to clients and they can quickly and easily follow all my content in a single place with their own reader."

Jim Quillen, Founder and Principal
Connect Social Media.

* * *

FriendFeed is a little different than most other social networking sites. It consolidates updates from various social networking sites and posts them on your homepage. With FriendFeed, you can create streams of information and customized feeds. For example, when Social Media expert, Chris Brogan was at Manchester Airport he posted a status line on Brightkite through his iPhone and FriendFeed automatically picked up the post.

You can see who is on which site and see their posts in a clear and concise manner. This site is known as an aggregator because it takes information from a lot of different places and presents it in one readable spot.

Through web crawling technologies, similar to those used by search engines, FriendFeed takes your username and automatically finds and broadcasts all of your public activity on that site.

This site provides complete control over who sees a feed. FriendFeed is either public or private and you can change preferences in the account page. If the FriendFeed is private, you approve every subscription request for their feeds, which will not be visible to anyone other than the approved friends. If choosing to make the FriendFeed public, anyone can subscribe to other users without requiring approval and their feeds will show up on the FriendFeed homepage.

This site is highly recommended for keeping track of all social networking sites and making updates from one central location. FriendFeed makes it easy to share videos, photos, blog sites and other social networking sites as well as link web sites and post profile updates.

You can also automatically import your address book from Gmail, Hotmail, Yahoo mail or AOL email accounts. This will enable you to know who is already using FriendFeed. Invite friends to FriendFeed, through the Facebook application. It automatically keeps friends in both Facebook and FriendFeed in sync.

You can also manually input email address and FriendFeed will send an invitation to those contacts.

Features on FriendFeed

Rooms

According to the company's web site, a room is like a mini FriendFeed for a particular subject or group of people. Everyone in the room can share information and leave comments that only people in that particular room can see. Unlike a chat room on AIM, this room stays open even when people are done chatting, unless you close it out.

Rooms can be public or private, as decided by the room's creator. If a room is public anyone can join. If it is private, the creator must invite or approve each member. And, as FriendFeed puts it, you can even have a room with a view by selecting "show this room's content" in my feed. This lets you view all of the activity from the rooms in your feeds. When creating a room, you can manage the settings and membership and invite new people to join.

Access all of the rooms in which you are a member or that you created by clicking on the rooms tab. FriendFeed also displays your room memberships along with your friend subscriptions (the friends to which you subscribe through Friendfeed). There's no limit to the number of rooms you can join or create.

Recently, I joined the Pepsi room. Pepsi has a number of representatives who post articles and stories. Their PR professional, Steve Rubel from Edelman PR, seems to write the majority of the feeds. Interestingly, the Pepsi representatives don't only promote Pepsi, they link various articles to the site. These articles are relevant to either social networking or marketing that might intrigue the people in their room. Some of Pepsi's marketing professionals also leave comments such as this one:

"I've seen a number of posts referring to social responsibility and wanted to get a sense of how social media can play a role in this area from participants. Pepsi and our corporate parent, PepsiCo, are actively engaged but I'd be interested in hearing your thoughts ..."

This kind of comment helps build and engage its followers. They also link to other bloggers who write about Pepsi. (Although, I have never seen any negative comments.) This helps create viral marketing to promote their message and brand.

MY 2 CENTS

I follow quite a few social media gurus. They write blogs and offer interesting ideas about using social media. Most are on FriendFeed, which enables me to learn from all of them in one place.

I like the way the rooms are set up and the discussions that take place in one location. I enjoy joining different rooms and interacting with people who share similar interests. I recently joined a Wordpress and a social media enthusiast room to gain more insight and initiate conversations that help me to build my community through the myriad of social media platforms.

hi5 Around the World
–hi5.com

"What makes hi5 fun is the ease by which you can add friends, send gifts and post events; all with one click on the same page. This shortens the time it takes to do such tasks and makes it much easier to keep your pages updated and current,"

Rick Eberle, Publicist

* * *

hi5 is a multicultural site with nearly 60 different languages and dialects. You can join various groups to develop friendships or business relationships. Those with businesses that market internationally, should consider registering with hi5.

hi5 is the most globally diverse social networking site in the world, with more than 80% of their users coming from outside of the United States. The hi5 site was designed for a global audience from the beginning and was the first social networking site to have many different languages.

Basic Info

Launched in 2003, hi5 helps its members stay connected with friends, family and business associates. Through the service (which adjusts to deliver information pertinent to each user), members link to people they've known throughout their lives, while making and maintaining new acquaintances as well. They use hi5 to share photos, send messages, express themselves with profile pages, join discussion groups, explore music and videos and more — making it easier to learn about what's happening in the lives of the people they care about, regardless of where they live or work.

Anyone can sign up for hi5, however, those who do must activate the account prior to getting started.

Personalizing Your Profile

About Me or Basic

The about me allows you to describe yourself in your own words. It also prompts you to list your first and last name, gender, birthday, hometown, looking to, relationship status and religion. Links at the top of the section send people to members' photos and allow members to include contact information, add a school or college and edit the interests section of their profile.

Visitors can also choose to display or hide some of their profile details on the edit page for this section. Click the link next to each field to select everyone can see this, my friends can see this or no one can see this. Be sure to click save to save new changes.

Interests

Interests allows you to include information about your personal interests or hobbies, favorite music, bands, television shows, movies and quotes.

Features on hi5

You will have a profile with the following features:

Recent Updates

Recent updates provides updates from your friends or groups. It also alerts you to the delivery of hi5 gifts, little objects that you can give to or receive from your friends on this site. Each hi5 gift comes wrapped, to open the gift click on the wrapped hi5 gift and see what is inside. Gifts include a unicorn, teddy bear or a kiss. You may send a gift to someone on their birthday as a gesture of kindness to build your relationship and strengthen your community.

Groups

Groups is a place to meet other hi5 members who share common interests. Join a group to meet new people and find other members with similar hobbies, interests and cultures. Members can also create their own groups and email them to other hi5 members.

Widgets

Widgets allow you to add all kinds of content to their profile -- slideshows, games, horoscopes and more. A slideshow may be helpful for new business development while some of the other applications may be used to engage the community.

Friends

hi5 offers many ways to make and invite friends, including:

- **Friend Suggestions** Located on the top of the home page, this feature lists members who are connected to you by your current friends. You can also access this feature by clicking the Find Friends link on the homepage.

- **Email Contact Importer** Use this feature to search your address books. You can also search your own address books on Hotmail, Yahoo, MSN, AOL, Gmail and other email providers available in their region by simply entering email address and password for that service and click the Find Friends button. This will lead you to a list of hi5 members in the email address book. You can also invite those on the list to be your hi5 friend by clicking add friends.

- **Invite A Friend** Access this feature directly from another member's hi5 profile. When viewing any hi5 member profile, click the add as a friend button below their primary photo to send an invitation.

- **Search** Use this feature to find hi5 members from your neighborhood or around the world.

- **List Of Friends** Check the list of friends featured on

friends' profiles. You will likely find people you would like to include as a friend.

Photos

Photo albums allow you to create, maintain and display groups of related photos. Using this feature, you can upload photos, create albums and display them to your friends on hi5.

To create a new photo album, click on my profile and then photos. Click the create album link from the left side navigation. Or, click the create a photo album link in the photo albums section of the profile page.

After selecting an album name and deciding who can view an album, click continue. Use one of the photo upload options to add photos to the new album. You can create up to 100 albums and each album can hold up to 250 photos. Total album capacity may not exceed 50 MB.

Scrapbook

A scrapbook is a collection of notes, comments and posts from other hi5 members. Scrapbooks are public and linked to a member's profile, allowing comments from anyone on hi5. The scrapbook also contains comments from friends who see you online now at hi5. The scrapbook topic can be changed at any time. A scrapbook does not include profile or photo comments. The scrapbook topic will also reflect your status to other members while on the site.

Journal

A journal entry is a part of your profile and allows you to tell Friends what they've been up to or create a public diary or life story. It includes a title, text and a photo. There is no character limit for journal entries.

Favorites

Similar to bookmarks, favorites are an easy way to save someone's hi5 profile or photo and return later to visit. Favorites are a private list of profiles and photos that do not appear on the profile for others to see. If you want to explore a profile of another member without adding that person as a friend, you can include the profile to your list of favorites.

Applications

Applications are games, surveys, maps and other customized gadgets, widgets and related features that you can add to your hi5 profile.

MY 2 CENTS

Since hi5 is an international site with thousands and thousands of users, it can benefit those business contacts out of the country. However, be aware that there are no unique or distinguishing features. It does the same thing as any of the other social media sites and doesn't really stand out from other available options. However, if you are doing business around the world, you may consider hi5 as the site in which you want to put your efforts.

Indenti.ca Tweets 2
-Identic.ca

"I really want to use Identi.ca more and to use it for more, but it's difficult. I haven't yet had a reason to make the jump away from Twitter. For a while, I had a bridge tool turned on that would take Identi.ca messages and automatically repost them to Twitter. That allowed me to just post a message once and it would get sent to both services. But only Twitterers would reply. Granted, I have a much larger community on Twitter, but still, at this point, I'm left in a position of wanting more out of Identi.ca -- not functionally, but wanting more people to be on Identi.ca."

Mike Keliher, **Client** Relations Manager
Fast Horse, www.fasthorseinc.com

* * *

Identi.ca is a microblogging service, where you can post short (140 character) notices that are broadcast to their friends and fans using the web, RSS or instant messages. It is also an international site that includes various languages and cultures.

There is one difference between Identi.ca and other microblogging sites. Those with an Identi.ca account can converse with friends on other social networking sites and these friends all interact with each other regardless of which accounts they belong.

Like many of the other social networking sites, Identi.ca has a Facebook integration page. Many people like Identi.ca better than Twitter because it's not as crowded.

Signing Up

You have the opportunity to create a nickname, which is your username for the site. Nicknames are available to followers. Every time you log onto the site, you will see your nickname.

The sign up application requires a name and email address, password for logging into the site, location and bio.

Personalizing Your Profile

The profile is where you will add posts as well as update personal information so the community knows more about them.

Features on Identi.ca

Each Identi.ca profile has the following features:

Statistics

Lists the amount of people who subscribe to the member and

those who are subscribed by the member. It also keeps track of the member's posts.

Current Status

Lists your status so that people know your activity and outlook at any given time.

Replies

Lists replies to others post and your subscribers reply to your posts.

Inbox/Outbox

Lists messages sent and received.

Favorites

Lists your posts and includes the time of each post.

Building a Community

Like many other social networking sites. Identi.ca offers several ways to build your community.

- You can invite friends by uploading their address book and sending an invitation to subscribe to your posts.
- Search for people on Identi.ca by their name, location or interests.
- Search for notices on Identi.ca by their contents.

MY 2 CENTS

Identi.ca is similar to hi5. Both are very clean, simple sites. Both list everyone's activity on a stream for you to review. Like hi5, Identi.ca is an international site. It enables you to talk with friends on other networks. What sets Identi.ca apart from Twitter is that it's not as crowded. I have nearly 5,000 followers on Twitter and the messages seem to get cluttered. I use Identi.ca when I microblog across all platforms and that has helped me gain exposure and visibility for the business on a global scale.

IncBizNet for Small Businesses
–IncBizNet.com

"Each of these social networking sites has their uses although they do crossover in some cases. As a whole they enable me to interact in my personal life and my business career in ways I could never do before. They have taken networking to a whole new level and allowed me to efficiently and effectively leverage the Internet. The speed with which you can expand your network is truly amazing."

Howard Silverstein, Consultant

* * *

Like *BusinessWeek*, *Inc.* magazine has also set up a social networking site. They see the value in creating a community and have done so successfully with IncBizNet. It is a social networking site designed exclusively for private U.S. companies.

In October of 2007, *Folio* magazine predicted before the site's launch, that IncBizNet "will become an extensive directory of U.S.-based private companies" with profile data regularly provided and updated by the companies themselves, including a press release newswire, blogs and community groups for entrepreneurs.

Signing Up

To sign up, state whether you are an individual, employee or company and whether your company is public or private. Individuals and public companies can currently see only limited profiles. In addition, registrants must enter full contact information, company information and so on.

On the homepage, you can search for companies, people, communities, events and products/services.

I tried for several months to access this social media site. When I tried to input my information, the site told me that I was already logged in. When I requested a new password via my email, I never received anything. I tried to do this several times on several different occasions and the results were the same. I was unable to access the site to explore and to see how it could help with business development.

MY 2 CENTS

This may be a great site if you can access it. Other sites offer better access and more detailed information. For example, if I want to learn more about the leaders of a particular company I visit ZoomInfo.com, a free source on the Internet that provides information about a professional businessperson. However, at the time of publishing, IncBiznet didn't offer me much so I don't have a way to evaluate the site.

Microblog on koornk
-koornk.com

*"I use koornk because I love the ability to keep
in touch with friends, partners, clients, industry
in quick and to the point messages,"*

Dawn Pigoni, Social Media Virtual Assistant
http://besocialworldwide.com

* * *

*"koornk started out as a development pet project intended to test
the company's technological platform. Since then it has evolved
into something completely unexpected – number of registered
users started growing in absence of any effort on the company's
side. Initial intent of creating an application that would
resemble Twitter but would offer localization and other cool new
features had to be surpassed. Today, koornk on top of all common
microblogging features offers many additional ones: detailed and
friendlier conversation tracking, enriched form for status updates*

(handy way of adding photos, links or multimedia), following and assigning topics, repeating others' status updates with one click etc.

As a microblogging application, koornk offers users to stay in touch with their friends but as a social network it also enables them to follow industry professionals and other relevant sources. By joining the right conversations, users get the privilege to receive or post the latest info on subjects of their interest first-hand. This enables them to create personal or business opportunities or just have some fun."

Maruša Grah, Corporate Communications Officer
Domenca d.o.o.

koornk is an international social networking site that aims to help members stay in touch with friends via short, quick microblogs. Those doing business across the world, may consider joining this social networking site. It also links with member's AIM and Twitter accounts.

koornk informs members on what everyone else is doing or considering. However, members must have friends in order to do this. koornk claims it will set you up with friends via their interests but at the time of this publishing, I have not been linked with anyone. (Does that mean I have no interests?)

Signing Up

Complete the sign up process, which requires name, username, password, email address, birthday, location and an optional cell phone.

Personalizing Your Profile

A profile is optional and can include a photo, your instant messenger username, other web sites, interests, an OpenID and links to other social networking sites. (An OpenID is a username and password that appears on all sites and is universal in opening the sites.)

Features on koornk

Followers

Follows is another word for friends. After establishing an account, search for other users by their interests, locations and so on.

Homepage

The homepage enables you to update your status, view recent posts, view replies, view mentions of their name and other members' status.

Members can also see their stats, number of followers, on the homepage.

MY 2 CENTS

As an international social networking site, koornk may benefit those who conduct business overseas. However, I don't find it as beneficial for people who are doing business locally because it doesn't have the same followers locally that some of the other microblog sites have. In addition, I found it difficult to build a community. I like the fact that the site is a microblog site. It's nice to read and write messages that have only 140 characters!

Link in on LinkedIn
–LinkedIn.com

"I have decided to ONLY use LinkedIn because I just about have time for one social networking site if used properly. It takes time, just like old time networking. If you tried to go to all the groups you would not be good for any one of them."

Steve Schwimmer
Renaissance Merchant Services
Chairman LI Advisory Board of Directors
Better Business Bureau

*   *   *

LinkedIn is one of the most popular business sites. Many people use LinkedIn for business purposes only. LinkedIn has evolved since its conception. You can see a stream of information from your community. You can connect and network with others by participating in polls, joining groups and sharing expertise.

The LinkedIn homepage provides a list of Network Updates, broadcasting what business contacts are doing and with whom they are connecting. It also lists the groups you have joined and updates on some of these groups. In addition, it lists news about some of the group members.

The homepage provides a very helpful news feed that is based on its members' interests. If you are interested in marketing, for example, you will find that LinkedIn provides all of the RSS feeds on marketing topics for your reading pleasure.

In addition, the homepage offers other valuable information like events in your area of expertise and job opportunities. It also provides an opportunity to ask and answer industry-related questions.

The more robust the profile, the more likely others will be drawn to learn about you. Make sure to list all work experience and current position, so that former colleagues and clients can easily find you. On the homepage, you can see if your profile is working by viewing how many page hits it received.

There are groups that you can join and various companies that you can search. Like Facebook and MySpace, LinkedIn has various applications that can enable members to promote their work and build a following. If a member decides to start a group, the member will be showcased as a thought leader. However, if you don't create a group, you may consider joining a group to meet new people and foster new relationships.

Perhaps one of the best features of LinkedIn is its application to help others, showcase expertise and receive valuable business advice. Business people both ask questions and you have an opportunity to respond to others' questions. Like Plaxo, this is truly a real business-oriented social networking site. Unlike Plaxo, LinkedIn has job searches, answers questions to problems or situations, like "what is a fair price for web hosting services?" and you can find out information about various companies.

Recently three old friends on LinkedIn contacted me -- one of them now lives in Chicago, another in Minnesota and the third in Denver.. I hadn't seen them in nearly twenty years. It was exciting to hear from them and by reconnecting, I broadened my business pool and increased my community outreach. Without LinkedIn, I don't think I would be in contact with them.

Signing Up

Complete the sign up application, including name and email address, password for logging into the site and location.

After signing up, customize your page to suit your needs. Click the boxes that relate to what you want to do with the site, for example, whether you're looking for a new job, reconnecting with colleagues, hiring employees and more. Select which types of subjects you want to be contacted with such as business proposals for companies and connecting with friends and colleagues.

Second and Third Degrees Away?

When you make a connection on LinkedIn, you will be connected with others in the 1st degree. Each of your contacts has their own contacts. This is called 2nd degree. The 3rd degree is contacts' contacts' contacts. You can ultimately meet anyone in the 2nd or 3rd degree with an introduction from someone in the 1st degree.

Personalizing Your Profile

The profile on this site is similar to that of a resume. Personalize the profile by uploading a photo of yourself using the LinkedIn prompts. This serves as the LinkedIn icon. Include information such as current job position, past job positions and education. The more information you provide, the more easily clients and colleagues – past and present – will find you.

Recommendations

Contact previous or even current employers or business colleagues on LinkedIn to request a recommendation of your work for your profile. This is useful when building your professional reputation and looking for potential jobs or clients. Through the recommendations tab, keep track of recommendation requests, recommendations sent and ones received.

Website

Post URLs for company websites, blogs and so on for contacts to view.

Public Profile

Make your profile public through the link provided by other social media sites, such as Twitter and Facebook.

Summary

Create a summary of work experience or company, as well as your specialty areas. This area is very similar to a resume and mission statement. Be as specific as possible.

Applications

Add applications to enhance your profile. Some of these applications include: slideshare presentations that allow you to upload and share presentations or a reading list by Amazon to share books you are reading with other LinkedIn members, Wordpress application to connect with your blog and polls survey the community.

Features on LinkedIn

Contacts

After creating a profile, Find/Invite contacts using LinkedIn's finder. There are six ways to add contacts, including:

1. Upload your address book from your personal email account and LinkedIn will find those who are on the site.

2. Input your old classmates names and LinkedIn will search its database for matches.

3. Post the URL link provided by LinkedIn so that contacts from other sites can find you. Include the link in your email signature and other social networking sites like Facebook.

4. Use the People Tab at the top of the homepage search for specific contacts.

5. Get in touch with past colleagues through the connections tab and placing information about previous jobs on the profile.

6. Invite contacts to your network through the Add Connections tab by entering their first and last name and email.

Introductions

Meet the people in your contacts' network by asking for an introduction on LinkedIn. This level of introduction serves as both an endorsement for you and an opportunity to meet someone who you really want to meet. However, I must state here that not everyone is comfortable making introductions and you can adjust settings if you don't want introductions.

Groups

LinkedIn has an abundance of groups to join in order to increase your number of contacts. Add groups to your profile that are of interest and can better serve you or your company.

To form a group, click on the 'Create a Group' and follow the step-by-step instructions.

Inbox

Send and receive messages from contacts through LinkedIn's email system. Click on the inbox tab and then compose the message. This method allows contact with other members while keeping messages private.

Jobs

Search for available jobs, posted by others by clicking on the Jobs tab. Enter the kind of job and location sought and LinkedIn then searches the database for matches.

Answers

Using the Answers tab, ask or answer questions, which are available for other users to see. LinkedIn stores any questions you have asked or answered for your records on your page.

Companies

Use this link to browse industries and companies on LinkedIn, which lists them according to your profile entries. This feature provides another way to make connections on the site. For example, you may find people you know listed in the breakdown. Or, you may find contact information for those you would like to meet at other companies.

Additional Information

While LinkedIn is a free social networking site, it does provide an option to upgrade to a paid account. Those who pay for the site gain access to additional networking tools and can deliver messages to people they know who have their privacy settings on to make sure they get the message.

MY 2 CENTS

I like LinkedIn. I find it useful for business. I've used the site to create groups and to promote different causes. I have also connected with business people that I haven't seen in years. I find that most business people are on this site. I also like the groups and the discussions on the site.

What I don't like about LinkedIn is that you need an introduction in order to connect with someone. In addition, making edits on the site are cumbersome. Those are my biggest complaints.

Professional Services on Plaxo
-Plaxo.com

"I am a big Plaxo fan. It is brilliant technology that provides a useful service -- groundbreaking service. Plaxo offers a network–based address book application that automates email address capture. Plaxo has grown to include social networking and life-streaming features but those are just commodity bells and whistles, which I rarely use. An ex–CEO of mine had 2000 contacts in his Outlook email address book. When I met him I had about 5. He used his as a Rolodex, making a conscious effort to record everyone's personal and professional data on a case-by-case basis. Perhaps he used an admin or assistant to key in all the data, but either way it took an awful lot of manual labor to create that contact database. And should his machine have ever crashed all his contacts work would have be gone. Enter Plaxo. Plaxo uses a software plug-in tied to your email client which allows users, in one click, to capture and save a new email address. And it saved to the Plaxo servers, never to be lost. If you choose to do

additional data entry, Plaxo allow that. Furthermore, Plaxo users who update their profiles on the Plaxo site synch up with users address books making contacts more accurate. If technology is to make life easier, Plaxo is a great technology. Thanks to Plaxo, I now have hundreds of contacts I didn't have before and when my laptop frazzled out last week and I had to have Windows reloaded, I lost nary a one. Plaxo is a great Web 2.0 business tool."

Steve Poppe, Managing Partner
What's the Idea? A Marketing Consultancy

* * *

Plaxo, an online address book and social networking service, provides automatic updating of contact information. You and your contacts store information on Plaxo's servers. When a contact edits his/her information, the updates appear in your address book. Once contacts are stored in the central location, you can access the address book from anywhere and list connections between contacts.

I like Plaxo for business. It has a profile page where you can talk about who you are and favorite activities. In addition, the status line enables you to share your latest news. I also like that Plaxo announces the updates I've made on Twitter and Flickr through the pulse stream (similar to what Facebook calls "the wall").

I have conducted a lot of business with people on Plaxo. Unlike Facebook's wall, which is open to everyone, the message sender is very user-friendly and private. Through Plaxo, I have personally met with several new contacts, which has broadened my prospect pool.

Signing Up

To sign up, register an email address and create a password. Enter first and last name, which is how followers will identify you. To maximize the ability to connect with contacts, provide country, birthday and gender. This helps to build common ground with connections. Once the username and password are created, activate the account through email.

Find People You Know

Plaxo enables you to find people you know through the following email accounts, including Gmail, Hotmail, AOL and Yahoo Mail. Add more people by sending co-workers, friends and family members invitations to join Plaxo.

Personalizing Your Profile

Create a profile by entering your work email and company name and adding the college/university and high school attended. This directs people to connect.

About Me

The About Me section allows you to describe yourself in your own words. Be sure to include some compelling information so that others are drawn to the site.

Here, you can enter your first and last names, gender, birthday, hometown, relationship status, religion, activities, interests, favorite music, TV/shows and books.

You can display or hide some of the profile details on the edit page for about me. For example, not everyone wants to include his or her birth year. Click the link at the end of the page to customize who can view the about me information.

Contact Information

Here, you can choose to list your contact information, including your work or personal data or both. You can also choose who can see your information and who cannot. To complete contact information, you enter your name, phone number (work or personal), AIM Screen name and email address. Think twice about the instant messenger username. Do you really want people instant messaging you at will?

Features on Plaxo

Pulse Stream

The pulse stream is a personal news page that automatically posts the updates that family, friends and business connections choose to share. To maximize the benefits of the pulse stream, these postings are visible to you once you log in.

Your pulse stream consists of all of the individual things that people have posted or shared with you that come together on your screen when you login.

Comments

Comments enables you to write notes and observations about your contacts' postings.

Photo Albums

Upload photos and create photo albums as well as tag photos of friends, family and colleagues.

My eCards

eCards are a great way to connect with contacts. eCards are online cards for birthdays, holidays and other occasions. They can be sent, received or scheduled online. While some cards are free, premium cards require a fee.

- Read and respond to comments on eCards you send to Plaxo members. Plaxo sends email notifications directing you to new comments on cards you sent to view and keep track of your sent, received and scheduled eCards. See which eCards you have already sent or have scheduled for future delivery and select new cards to keep the mix interesting.

- Control who can see your sent eCards. To allow other people who are connected to the recipient to see your sent eCard, send it as a Social eCard. If you only want the recipient to see your eCard, send it as a private eCard.

Connections

Connections enables you to find friends and colleagues on Plaxo. This page provides a list of friends of people to connect with.

Address Book

The address book stores the contact information of everyone you know. It also:

- Synchronizes with other address books so that every time you delete or modify a contact in one of them, the change will reflect across all the address books you are synching with, including Outlook, Google, LinkedIn, Outlook Express, Hotmail, Windows Mobile, Mac, AOL, Windows Mail and your cell phone.

- Allows contacts to update their own information directly in your address book. When a contact changes his or her address and updates it in Plaxo, that change will reflect in your address book.

Calendar

The calendar racks events by synching with the information already listed in your Yahoo, Gmail or Outlook accounts.

Fan Pages

Become a fan of a favorite TV show and watch full episodes online for free, express opinions with other fans and share episodes with friends.

Groups

Groups lets you limit sharing to a select set of people. By creating or joining a group in Plaxo, you can easily share information (feeds, messages, photos and more) with just that group of people. Anyone in the group can view, comment and share with everyone else in the group.

Messages

Messages allows you to send and receive messages from other member's address book.

Share Videos, Photos and Reviews

Because this site is used for business people, consider shaping the videos and photos to attract clients.

Link Web Sites

Link several different web sites or you provide a link to your home page.

Link Blog Sites

Link several different blog sites or provide a link to your home page.

Link Other Social Media Sites to the Plaxo Account

Plaxo supports many other social networking sites like Twitter, Bebo, Tumblr and more.

Update Your Profile

Whenever you want to add or subtract something from your existing profile.

Update Your Calendar on Plaxo

They have a great calendar on the site that business owners can use as their daily calendar.

Address Book

The address book can be used all the time for business. Friends who are already on Plaxo are included in the address book. However, you can also add other contacts to the address book as well.

Plaxo is recommended for new business networking, meeting potential clients, connecting with current friends and clients, checking updates on others schedules and so on.

MY 2 CENTS

Plaxo has not gained the publicity that LinkedIn enjoys, but it is used far more. I know this because I created a networking group in New York City. I wanted to see if I could meet my virtual friends in a real world setting by scheduling a meet-up at a predetermined time and place. I created three groups – one on Facebook, one on LinkedIn and one on Plaxo. Do you know which one had the most responses? Facebook came in first with 80 people, Plaxo second with 40 people and LinkedIn last with 13 members.

I like that Plaxo enables me to connect with anyone and everyone, unlike LinkedIn, because with LinkedIn the member needs an introduction with someone they don't know before connecting. I like that it simplifies my life by updating my address book whenever one of my contacts changes jobs or addresses, a very useful feature. Plaxo is definitely worth a look and worth opening an account!

Plurk for Perks!
-Plurk.com

"Plurk is fun. I like the way posts scroll across the screen in a horizontal matter. The Karma points are fun to try to increase. Not much interaction from what I've seen but the people on there seem to post relevant things not mindless drivel. I like the expansion of posts to read. This is a fun site to play on."

Gary Unger, Creative At Large
www.GaryUnger.com

* * *

Plurk is geared for teens and twentysomethings. It claims that once you use it, it will become addicting. Those who market to this age group may consider joining this site. I tested out the addiction hypothesis to see if it were true. Needless to say, I did not get addicted.

Plurk is a microblogging portal that allows you to send updates (otherwise known as Plurks) through short messages or links, which can be up to 140 text characters in length.

Updates are on the your home page through a timeline that lists all status changes received in chronological order and delivers them to other users who sign up to receive them. You can respond to other's updates on Plurk.com, by instant messaging or by text messaging.

Signing Up

Create a "nickname." This will be available to those who follow you. Complete the sign up application, which requires a name, email address, password for logging into the site, birthday and location.

Personalizing Your Profile

Create a profile and include a photo. This will serve as a Plurk icon. In addition, include information about yourself (no more than 250 characters). The background, timeline and dashboard colors can all be changed.

Features on Plurk

Features and Technology

Plurk's interface makes it easy to scroll through updates on the timeline; which is presented in a horizontal form. You can post new messages by selecting a host of optional qualifiers, one-word verbs used to represent a thought (for example "feels," "thinks," "loves" and so on). There are also advanced features such as sending updates only to a subset of friends; posting updates on events that took place earlier in the day; and sharing images, videos and other media.

Timeline

Track you and your followers' Plurk posts by date and time with this feature. Timelines can be private or public.

Friends

Use Plurk's friend finder to find and invite friends. Upload address book from your email account and Plurk will find and contact those who are on the site. In addition, input your username from Twitter, and Plurk will search their database for matches. Plurk provides a URL link so that your friends from other sites can follow you. Post links to your Plurk account in your email and other social networking sites like Twitter or Facebook. If needed, remove friends from your profile at any time by using the block friend tab.

Fans

Boost your karma (see below) rating through fans. Fans are Plurkers who follow your timeline (status updates/messages) but have not been added as a friend.

Karma

Generate karma by posting Plurks, responding to other Plurks and getting people to follow you. The more karma you get, the more you can add to your profile.

Every Plurker has his or her own karma value. It is recalculated each day and ranges within these intervals:

- 0.00 to 21.00: You are in the state of creation
- 21.00 to 41.00: You are in the state of maintenance
- 41.00 to 61.00: You are enlightened
- 61.00 to 81.00: You are so close to Plurk Nirvana
- 81.00 to 100.00: You have reached Plurk Nirvana!

Some tips on getting more karma:
- Update your profile (picture, location, birthday and more)
- Quality Plurking each day
- Respond to other Plurkers
- Inviting your real friends to join you on Plurk

What will lower your karma:
- Requesting friendships that get rejected
- Getting unfollowed by friends
- Spamming other users
- Laying dormant on Plurk for a long period

Stay active by commenting or by sharing information. Those who spam on Plurk lose friends and generate negative karma.

Stars

Enhance your profile with stars, which are added to your profile as an incentive for inviting friends to join Plurk.
- Silver #10 friends added
- Gold #25 friends added

- Red #50 friends added

MY 2 CENTS

Through the 17 years that I have owned and operated my business, I have worked with many people under the age of 30. It's amazing how many of them believe in karma. The language and philosophies of this site resonates with the millennium generation (people born from 1980's to today) or what many are calling the digital natives. To market to this age group or seek a job candidate, I may consider posting on Plurk.

Spoke for Business Folk
-Spoke.com

"Someone posted something about my company on Spoke attributing a VP that I never heard of. His name is still there. I have been complaining for months now. We sent emails every week with no reply. I can't even log in and remove the name. We're so annoyed with the site and their customer service!"

Fran Bidderman Gross, President & CEO
Advantage

*   *   *

According to the site, more than 40 million business people and 2.3 million companies use Spoke. Spoke connects with anyone in the Network, regardless of whether he or she is a member. Spoke is a great tool to grow professional networks and connect with the right people.

This site is used for those in sales, business development, marketing, recruiting, business research and executives as well as those seeking a job. Both individuals and groups at large and small companies use Spoke's connection resources to accelerate their new business development efforts as well as sustain critical business relationships.

With Spoke, you can find individual contributors, managers, directors and executives at target companies along with the information to access them including name, title, phone, address, job history, profiles, community comments and potential business connections.

Signing Up

There are three steps to getting started on Spoke – building your profile, building your network and building new relationships.

Building your profile

Include a photo and some background information. Introduce yourself to the Spoke community by telling members who you are, what you do and what you can add by being a friend. In addition, enter education, work experience, interests as well as corporate web sites and blogs.

Build Your Network

At first, I tried to build my network but was directed to a page that said that this function was unavailable. When I went to the site weeks later, I realized that this function does not work with an email account that is linked to a web site. Therefore, I was unable to use it.

Build New Relationships

Find individuals at companies by entering key information as prompted.

For an additional fee, you can upgrade your membership and enjoy tools for lead generation and sales prospecting. However, since I don't really use this program often, I opted out.

MY 2 CENTS

I have a Spoke account and thought that this was going to be my favorite site when I started to look into it. I primarily use the site for microblogging. I don't use it to build business because I don't find it user-friendly like some of the other sites.

Tumblr for Blogging
-Tumblr.com

"I maintain three Tumblogs. Two are for business and one is personal. I also must ad that I own Doth Brands, which is a graphic design studio specializing in branding and identity. We have many of our clients use Tumblr for their blogging platforms. Many business owners are baby-boomers and we've found that Tumblr is the easiest blogging platform for them to pick up."

Cole Imperi, Owner
Doth Brands

* * *

When searching for Tumblr.com, don't make the same mistake I made and type in Tumbler.com, because if you do, you will end up on Travis Tumbler's site, which sells tumbling cups. You will shake your head and walk away!

Tumblr, which is a play on the word, tumblelog, is a variation of a blog, except instead of entries, you make short posts or microblogs like on Twitter. It is ideal for someone who wants to be on a social networking site or wants to have a blog, but does not have time to constantly update or make new entries.

Signing Up

This is a very simple registration. You enter your email address, creates a password and a blogpage URL.

Personalizing Your Profile

Customize a tumblelog as if you were customizing a blog or MySpace page. Customize tumblelogs with the following:

Information

Give the tumblelog a title, add information and upload a portrait to the tumblelog.

Theme

Choose the theme for the tumblelog from a list of different customized themes already created or for comfortable hand-coding HTML to create your own theme.

Appearance

Modify the appearance of your tumblelog by selecting the color of the page. Choose the default color or change the colors on a page for each of the following items:

- Background
- Text

- Link

- Header

- Date Text

- Date

- Image Border

- Image Background

- Previous/Next Tab

- Footer Border

Advanced Tailoring

Tailor your site by changing time zones, advertising on the tumblelog and adding custom CSS (cascading style sheets which adds style to web pages or blogs).

Features on Tumblr

Your Dashboard

The Tumblr dashboard is your profile and is very easy to navigate.

Dashboard Features:

- **Show All Posts** Posts recently made on the your tumblelog. Select this feature to see who is following you and who you are following. Follow a tumblelog by visiting any of its web pages and clicking the follow icon in the upper right corner of the page. Or enter the URL, username or email of a tumblelog.

- **Add a Text Post** Insert a comment on a blog or wall post. It is the most basic element to add to a tumblelog.

- **Upload a Photo Post** Upload any photo through prompts from the website. Photos can supplement other text.

- **Add a Quote** A favorite quote or expression to the tumblelog.

- **Add a Link** Favorite web sites, blogs and company web site to the tumblelog.

- **Add a Chat Post** A dialogue held, had with someone or overheard.

- **Add an Audio Post** A podcast or another recording from your files or for embedding into your tumblelog from another web site.

- **Add a Video** A video podcast or another video from your files or for embedding it into your tumblelog from another web site.

- **Bookmarklet** Anything that you find interesting online including, videos, images, music and more. Click on the share on tumblr bookmarklet, which then tumbles the snippet directly. The result is a varied string of media ranging from links and text, to pictures and videos and takes very little time and effort to maintain.

- **Feeds** Import posts from up to five other sites through feeds. In the spirit of original work, if importing other people's content, your account will be suspended.

MY 2 CENTS

This site is recommended for CEO's or executives who have little time to blog but want to get their companies name and brand recognition on the Internet. I like that Tumblr is a microblog site and delivers short bits of information. Its big typeface is an added bonus for those of us needing reading glasses. The site is clean and well organized. It's definitely worth a look.

Tweet in Twitter Land
-Twitter.com

"I like Twitter because it helps me keep in touch with my family in Pennsylvania. I put a Twitter widget on my blog so my parents can keep track of the spur of the moment things they would otherwise miss. Moving upstate New York was not easy, but through Twitter, I get to stay in contact with friends and acquaintances. It's also a sanity saver for a stay-at-home mom who would otherwise have little adult contact during the day."

Robin Lamb, Freelance Writer

*   *   *

Twitter, a free microblogging site, has more than 3 million users and its tweeter base is growing every day! It is one of the most powerful social media sites out there today. The site allows you to send and read others updates (otherwise known as tweets), which are text posts of up to 140 characters in length. Twitter is one of my favorite sites because thought leaders, CEO's of huge corporations and media people use it regularly to get their message and brand out in the public eye.

On Twitter, I connect with editors and reporters. I post microblogs seeking guest bloggers and recommendations and I received them almost instantly. No strings attached!

Twitter allows you to follow people. I like to follow other social media gurus so that I have the opportunity to learn new things. I also follow reporters and editors to find out what types of stories they are working on and I follow corporations to see how they are utilizing Twitter for their marketing purposes. Updates are displayed on the your profile page and delivered to other users who decide to follow you.

Twitter is used by large organizations, including Cisco Systems, JetBlue, Whole Foods Market, Dunkin' Donuts and Starbucks. Most of the bigger brands are on Twitter.

Interestingly, the Los Angeles Fire Department put Twitter to work during the October 2007 California wildfires and NASA used it to break the news of the discovery of what appeared to be ice water on Mars by the Phoenix Mars Lander. Terror attacks in India are reported widely on Twitter and 10,000 young Moldavians used Twitter to organize protests against Moldova's Communist leadership. News outlets such as CNN and the BBC use Twitter to disseminate breaking news or provide information feeds for sporting events.

One of President Barack Obama's claim to fame is his innovative use of social networking and technology especially Twitter. Notably, President Obama engaged young people through

Twitter, which helped win the 2008 U.S. presidential election campaign.

The University of Texas at San Antonio College of Engineering uses Twitter to relay information to students on events at the campus, research and other student's accomplishments.

When Lance Armstrong lost his bicycle after a major race in California, he sent out a message via Twitter. Everyone including the police received the message and within hours, his bicycle was found!

Signing Up

To join Twitter, create a username, which will be available to followers on the site. If later you decide to change the username you can do so without losing the followers, thanks to Twitter's well thought-out software.

Complete the sign up application, which requires a name, email address, password for logging onto the site and location.

Personalizing Your Profile

Create a profile and uploaded a photo. This serves as your Twitter icon. Include information about yourself (no more than 140 characters). Stick with the stock backgrounds or change it through the design tab located on the settings tab. Include a link to your personal blog or homepage. Make the profile public (allowing anyone to follow you) or private (allowing only those who you are friends with access to your tweets).

Features on Twitter

On the homepage, there is a stream of various microblogs. Here, you will have an opportunity to either join in the conversation or create your own conversation. On the right side of the screen under your username, you will notice the amount of people following you and those you are following. In addition, if you click on the updates, you will see all your microblogs.

The @ next to your username is where messages about you are located. The direct messages section is where all the direct messages are located. These are messages that only you see. The messages sent to @ your username, can be seen by everyone on Twitter.

On Twitter, you also have an area to bookmark your favorite microblogs to reference back. If for example, you saw a post that you would like to keep you add it to your favorite section.

There is also a Facebook interface where you can see all of your friends' status lines from Facebook. In addition to a search feature, there are also trending topics that you can join in to have a discussion about a specific topic, i.e., the Swine Flu, the television show "24" or the economy.

Interestingly, I was reading the Buzzmachine a blog about social media. The writer talked about how he was on an Amtrack train and it got stopped. He went on Twitter to see what was going on and heard that there were major delays. Someone else who was on Twitter also microblogged about the situation and they ended up getting off the train and carpooling back to New York. He said he even ended up doing business with the guy.

Friends

After creating a profile find and invite friends using Twitter's friend finder. Upload the address book from your personal email account and Twitter will find those who are on the site. However, you need to select people you want to follow. Input friends' usernames from other social networking sites and Twitter will search their database for matches. Twitter provides a URL link so that friends from other sites can follow you. It also appears on Google searches so that people can find you. Post the link in emails and other social networking sites. Friends can be removed from the profile at any time by using the block friend tab. In addition, private messages can be sent to a friend using the "direct message" tab.

Phone Application

Link Twitter to your mobile phone to continue to see your friends' updates as well as post your updates. This gives you the ability to live blog and is a great way to communicate about travels. For example, @Whiteonrice linked to a trip they took to Vietnam. Every day, they would post new microblogs about their adventures. Whenever I am at the airport or traveling, I also post microblogs about my travels through my phone.

What else can be done with Twitter?

Business leaders can post information about new products or services and link to a web site, blog or media room for further information. They do this to brand their service or product and drive web traffic. Leaders link their tweets to their blogs and web pages.

Some people like to share resources on Twitter because it builds their reputation, helps build relationships and makes them seem like the experts in their field. They post a message and link to an interesting article that they found on the web, some even link to their own web sites and blogs.

You can also enjoy other activities on Twitter, which are enhanced by the following applications:

- **Twitpic** Post a photo on Twitpic and then share the Twitpic link via Twitter.

- **Twhirl** Keep Twitter open on your desktop all day in real time. The messages are on continuous scroll and you will see the message instantaneously.

- **Tipjoy** Send small amounts of cash to charities and businesses across Twitter and then tweet about the payment as another way to share news about donations and purchases.

- **Twibs** A list of businesses on Twitter with links to their Twitter accounts. This enables you to learn about new products and promotions. It also enables businesses to build a following.

- **TweetDeck** Desktop software so that you can organize your tweets into columns, such as @replies, direct messages, groups and keyword searches.

- **Twitterholic** Ranks Twitter users by number of followers. The more followers, the more you are considered an expert.

- **Twitturly** Tracks which URLs are most popular on

Twitter based on how many times they've been shared by Twitter users.

- **Monittor** Tracks keywords and trends on Twitter. If you are a reporter or blogger, for example, you may use this to see what people are saying about a particular subject matter.

- **Bubbletweet** Add video to your tweet.

- **ExecTweets** Follow top business executives on Twitter.

- **TwiVite** Aimple event manager application for Twitter. It's similar to an Evite (online invitation) that managers guests to an event.

- **Twellow** Online database of Twitterers organized by industry. It works very similar to a traditional yellow pages.

With Twitter so new and growing so rapidly, there was bound to be some controversies. One such instance includes re-tweets. A re-tweet is a microblog created by one user and then repeated more than once. Many people were upset because they saw the same tweet over and over again. I follow nearly 5,000 people and nearly 5,000 people follow me. There are some who follow thousands and thousands follow them. How could you capture all the information on twitter if you follow that many people? That is why re-tweets are useful, especially when the content is worthy of a look!

Here's a list of people to consider following:

- @Tweetreplies suggests people that you should follow.

- @GuyKawasaki is a social media guru and offers a lot of advise in the social media world.

- @Scobleizer is a technology enthusiast and blogger and offers a wide range of interesting information focusing on social media.

- @Ducttape is duct tape marketing and offers users an opportunity to learn new marketing techniques and strategies.

- @Hilary25 is my username on Twitter.

- @HJMT is my PR firm on Twitter.

While a wide variety of businesses use Twitter to market products and services, some larger companies in particular use Twitter to follow those at the office. Their staffers microblog about what they are doing all day keeping the lines of communication open at work.

Many use hashmarks before a word on Twitter to follow a conversation. For example, every Monday night there is a Journalism and PR chat. At 7pm, you can do a search for #JournChat and you will be connected to the chat. Questions are asked and it makes it relatively easy to follow a conversation. Many conferences and seminars are using these hashmarks for attendees to give remarks or to post comments about the session.

To search for any topic or company, go to search.twitter.com. You will be directed to a search engine where you can locate any topic, organization or person on Twitter.

Still others use it to target online media outlets and make them aware of different resources available to them. For example, at HJMT COMMUNICATIONS, LLC, we microblog "pitches" to the media via Twitter and direct the media back to the HJMT Newsroom.

MY 2 CENTS

I love Twitter. I highly recommend it. It's a program that I use every day and keep open all the time. I learn new things on Twitter. I stay in touch with my community and I conduct business on Twitter by making initial contacts with people and then meeting them in person. I also talk with other people in my field about shared information. The other night I went online and found a conversation about emerging trends in the PR and journalism fields, which I wouldn't have tapped into nearly as rapidly without Twitter.

Yammer for Internal Use -Yammer.com

"At Angelsoft, we use Yammer to communicate among the half dozen people on our sales and business development teams. Since our average Twitter follow/follower numbers are in the 400-500 range, we needed a way to isolate our business messaging from the general-purpose tweet-traffic. Yammer provides a clean interface, good tool set and professional feel that makes it work well for us in a business context."

David S. Rosc, CEO
Angelsoft

* * *

Yammer is a site to use for internal purposes. It's a great site to use at work to communicate with staff and to track what everyone is doing and working on at any given time. When signing up, you will be asked who you work with and who you manage. This way Yammer can send out emails to those folks to get them on the site.

Signing Up

Upon signing up, you will be asked to enter a valid company email address, full name and job title. Then a password will be created. Once signed up, coworkers, managers and supervisors will receive an email to join Yammer.

Personalizing Your Profile

Home Page

On the company's home page, you can view feeds (messages to coworkers) sent and messages received.

Edit the profile, change the profile picture and add mobile phones to the profile from this page.

Members

This feature shows your network. It also lists followers and pending invitations. Under the more tab, the following tabs appear:

- **Links** Add links to this page. It lists all links that are within the network.
- **Files** Upload files to share with co-workers.
- **Images** Upload photos of the company and its employees.
- **Profile** Upload your photo, which becomes your identity for the company's network. Include interests, the current position at the company and personal information.

Company Branding

The program enables businesses to upload the company logo to their Yammer Page. The logo replaces the company name at the top of the page. This can be removed at any time. By having the company logo on every page, this helps build employee pride and helps instill a sense of teamwork and togetherness.

Features on Yammer

Although anyone with a valid business email address can start a free Yammer network, companies can claim their network by paying for optional administrative (admin) tools. These include:

Manage Content and Members

The administrator can remove a member from the network or delete any message.

Password Policies

The administrator can determine the minimum character length and complexity for passwords.

Session Settings

The administrator can require email confirmation when logging in from a new browser.

IP Range

The administrator can assign an IP (Internet Protocol) range, restricting access to the office network or VPN (virtual private network).

Custom Logo

The administrator can brand the network by uploading the company logo to appear at the top of every page.

Assign Admin Privileges

The administrator can grant additional administrative privileges to any user on the network.

Additional Information

Administrative privileges cost $1 per month per member of the company network. There is a free 30-day trial period for administrative privileges, after that the administrator of record will be billed.

MY 2 CENTS

The HJMT staff and I used Yammer for about a month. I wanted to test drive the program. I found that only two or three people were updating it and it became more of a burden than anything else. I did like the program and would use it if I had a huge staff. With a smaller staff, I already know where everyone is and it became more time consuming than anything else. Otherwise, the site was clean and very user-friendly. For companies that have remote workers and freelancers, Yammer is highly recommended.

YouAre Where?
-YouAre.com

"My concern with so many sites, like Seth Godin said when we heard him speak, is that you need to choose the sites that work best for you and place your efforts there. Just like networking in the physical world, you can't be everywhere, there will be social networking services -- your blog, a couple of social networking sites -- that are more important to you and that receive more of your time and care,"

Arthur Germain, Principal
Communication Strategy Group

* * *

YouAre is a free service in which you share activities, interests and professional profiles with friends and colleagues -- and anyone else you want to connect with. However, with YouAre, you need a personal invitation to become a member. Upon visiting the web site, log in with an email address to get invited to join. It takes a few days before you get an invitation but in the meanwhile, the site directs you to its blog for more information about the site. By the time, you get the invitation, you know how to manage the site from reading the blog.

Features on YouAre

YouAre is a microblogging site. You communicate in posts of 140 characters and can share text, video and images. You can control updates received to include only your real life friends, online friends, acquaintances, co-workers, colleagues and family. You can import content from YouTube, Flickr and Delicious (social bookmarking site). In addition, you can also include video and pictures from your cameras. Further, you can promote professional skills and services.

On the profile, you can list your web site, blog site, education, work experience and more. There is also an area where you can post a 140-character synopsis of who you are. The interesting thing about this site is that you can find other professionals in a target areas and fields. In addition, you can implement filters to talk with key people. The site has an easy help menu that answers any and all questions.

MY 2 CENTS

I liked the site because I find it easy to use and the site's colors are attractive and appealing to me. However, I was annoyed that it took nearly a week to get an invitation to become part of it. Before I even gave it a chance, I lost interest. It does have good features and a solid foundation and perhaps you will get an invite faster than I did.

Audio and Video to Get Your Message Out

*"I have a recycling glass business and on our home page
are YouTube videos of the show "How it's Made" featuring
a segment on recycling, how glass is made and creating
asphalt. We posted that on YouTube on 6/12/08 and without
any advertising or marketing, we have over 13k views
on one video. Since our profile has our company name and
a link to our website, we are able to drive traffic to it and
free advertising, http://www.gogreenwithglass.com."*

Eric Duchin
Go Green with Glass

*"YouTube helps me bring in new visitors to my site. I posted a
video on a waterfall in the Smoky Mountains and within a
week, more than 150 new people had watched the video and
many of those people went to my website. Social media works
well when you work a number of the sites/tools together. I use
Twitter to push to my blog and I use message board comments to
push to the blog as well. Then I use the blog to push to message*

boards and other social media sites, like my YouTube or Twitter accounts. Together, they all work to help more people find out about what I'm doing online. This helps me get information out to people who are interested in the Smoky Mountains."

Raymond Owens
www.GoSmoky.com

* * *

In addition to blogs, microblogging and social networking sites, it is important to continue to gain exposure and visibility by having your company appear on an audio or video podcast or both.

What is a Podcast?

A podcast is an audio news release or interview show that is controlled by you, the consumer. It sounds like a radio show and gives concrete information about a particular topic. It must not be self-promotional. If it is, people won't be interested in listening. Some entities that do podcasts well include:

- http://www.blogtalkradio.com/smallbiztrends -- Blogtalk Radio has many different shows for small businesses and on social media trends.

- http://www.podcastalley.com/ -- Podcast Alley includes the top podcasts on many different subjects and topics. By going to the site, you can listen to dozens of podcasts in all categories.

Podcasts are helpful in generating viral marketing. Use podcasts on an RSS feed, on iTunes, on your own web site and other aggregators.

Effective podcasts feature a spokesperson, whether an articulate staff member or the owner, discussing the company, product or service. In others, a spokesperson introduces the company, product or service and then someone on your staff speaks. Each week you can record a new introduction and end with a teaser, inviting listeners to stay tuned for next week's podcast. Having a voice behind your product or service is important to connect with future consumers.

Podcasts don't have to be slickly polished. There is definitely something about ones that are authentic because they instill trust. Professional is something else. Try to strike a balance between authentic and professional.

When formulating a podcast, it's important to have an outline or a script to keep you on target. It's helpful to put some type of music in the background based on type of industry and podcast subject. There is a host of free music online. Explore and determine which one suits your podcast best. Music keeps the interview on pace and on track. It also helps to keep the listener focused on the interview.

Why a Podcast?

According to *Podcasting News*, the US audience for podcasts will double within the next two years. They say by 2012, there will be an audience of 65 million listeners.

How to Make a Podcast

A podcast can be easily produced with an MP3 recorder, a lavaliere microphone and some editing equipment. Editing software can be found free on the Internet. One popular software on the market is called Audacity but you can also use Garage Band, which is frequently found on Macbooks.

Think about the location where you will record the podcast. Do you want to record at the office with the background noise? And, if you do, will that add to the charm of the podcast?

Editing does take time, so be patient. It could take a few hours and a few tries to get it right. In addition, you may consider taking out all the "ummms." Or, you may leave in the "ummms," to make it seem more real and spontaneous. Try to keep the points consistent.

Once you finalize it, it's time to post. Don't forget to microblog about the new post so that people who don't use your RSS feed can hear it and you continue to build your community.

Promote the podcast via your blog, social networking sites and even consider posting a press release in your newsroom. The more listeners the better and the more you include podcasts into your social media marketing program, the higher your SEO ranking will be.

Video Podcasts

YouTube and other online vehicles that showcase videos are all the rage right now. Video podcasts are powerful tools to getting a message out. They can appear on all of your social networking sites and like television, they draw the viewer in. The best video podcasts are those that are raw and authentic. Polished podcasts don't cut it because they look professionally done and then tend to be unbelievable because they look too much like commercials.

Before you start, purchase an inexpensive camcorder. When I first started to do video podcasts, I spent around $3,000 for a good camera that had high definition quality. However, podcasters can now purchase a Flip Video camera for just under $100. The Flip is portable, lightweight and looks like a digital camera.

The Flip Video plugs right into the computer's USB port, which connects electronic devices into the computer. The software is downloadable.

Editing is the tricky part. Free editing software is available online making the process relatively simple. But be warned that podcast editing requires a lot of time and patience.

There are endless possibilities to incorporate into a video. Some use these podcasts as a video log or Vlog, which they record regularly. To see an example of a Vlog, go to YouTube and put in Vlog in the search. Quite a few Vlogs will appear on your page to review.

Some use videos to promote a product, contests or upcoming events. Some use them to get a message out to the community, for example, a superintendent of a school district may talk about school updates to parents.

One video site to watch is Seesmic. Seesmic is an online community where you can connect through online video conversations. Post a video through Seemic's web site or with a mobile phone or a computer. Others will post video in reply. I love Seesmic. I think that the site has a lot to offer. I use it to ask questions and talk with social media experts around the world. I also see Seesmic as the future of Facebook. People love to watch people in person, that's why television became more popular than radio in the 1940's and 1950's. Within the next five years, I can see more of these social media sites turning to video as a way of communication.

Video is a very engaging medium. Consider SKYPE, a free software that allows you to make phone calls over the Internet and at the same time view live video feed. Why are these so popular? Because people want to see the person they are listening to or talking with. It's more engaging and ultimately, I suspect these will gain more popularity as time goes by.

MY 2 CENTS

Podcasts and video podcasts are important in every social media plan. When made right, they help create viral marketing and get your product or service noticed. At HJMT COMMUNICATIONS, LLC, we try to have either a podcast or video podcast every week. We link them to our web site, YouTube site and other places throughout the Internet to get as much exposure and recognition for our services.

Many companies have succeeded by using audio and video podcasts. Blendtec is a great example. As a result of their videos, sales went up 700%.

The most important thing to remember is, you must do something different and be creative to go viral. Remember that whatever video you produce must be something that people will share.

Watch YouTube Regularly?

"I was laid off from an Internet marketing position in September 2008. Even though I consulted with Fleishman-Hillard, Hill & Knowlton and Edelman/PR, I didn't have agency experience listed on my web site so it was hard to get noticed. A friend of mine suggested I do YouTube instructional videos and I went one step further by creating a series of skits called "PR Puppet Theatre" where I offered PR advice to my daughter's puppets. I taped five skits and sent to CNBC correspondent, Jane Wells who immediately posted it on her Funny Business blog, calling "must-see entertainment/education for every PR flack." She liked the skit so much that she posted another a few weeks later. I used her endorsement and told potential employers, if I can get a cheesy puppet show on CNBC, think of what I can do for your clients. Funny thing is, the site has had less than 500 hits, but the fact that I did it and promoted it on CNBC is one reason why I was hired to my current job. The link to the site: http://www.youtube.com/prpuppettheatre."

David Moye, Media Relations Manager
Alternative Strategies

*   *   *

YouTube is one of the most popular sites on the Internet today. Founded in February of 2005, this video sharing website is also used for social networking. When executed properly, a video on YouTube will certainly go viral.

YouTube allows millions of people to discover, watch and share originally created videos. It provides a forum for people to connect, inform and inspire others across the globe and acts as a distribution platform for original content creators and advertisers large and small.

Who watches YouTube? According to the YouTube fact sheet located on the site, most people watching YouTube are between 18-55, evenly divided between males and females and spanning all geographies. The majority of the users go to YouTube weekly or more often and share videos with friends and colleagues.

Do you remember lonelygirl15? According to the *New York Times*, she posted videos on YouTube regularly. Every day she sat in her bedroom and talked about the trials and tribulations of a home-schooled teenager of religious parents. It became one of the most popular videos on YouTube. Later, it was discovered that lonelygirl15 was an actress who graduated from New York Film Academy who had teamed up with film directors and a screenwriter. The team succeeded in attracting millions of devotees and coverage in *The New York Times*, which only helped their Hollywood careers. The scenario brings to life how enterprising people can use YouTube to build a following.

YouTube allows people to easily upload and share video clips both on YouTube as well as across the Internet through other web sites, mobile devices, blogs and email. YouTube is a user-friendly community. Viewers watch current events, relive their favorite TV shows, find videos about their hobbies and interests and discover new artists and filmmakers.

Signing Up

Anyone can sign up for a YouTube account and upon registration those who do are given their very own channel.

You can tailor your accounts for branding purposes by:

- Customizing their homepage.
- Changing the playback setup.
- Using the mobile setup to access YouTube by phone or to download video directly from phone.
- Setting up a blog.

Features on YouTube

YouTube offers many features to enhance the viewing and sharing experience. These basic features include the ability to:

- **Upload videos** write a title and description of the video and give the video "tags" or keywords for people to find the video.
- **Favorites** Mark videos as favorites.
- **Play Lists** Create your own customized playlist.
- **Search** For friends with similar interests and add friends to grow one's network.

- **Post a Bulletin** Announce your status or which video you are currently watching.

- **Link to a YouTube Video** Copy the URL from the browser. Then paste it into the web site or blog. Depending on the blogging or web design software, it may make the link clickable automatically. You cannot link it so when you click on the video it goes to the web site. Also, keep in mind that in order to look at private videos and to comment on videos you must have YouTube account.

MY 2 CENTS

YouTube is a great way to get your message out! Companies use YouTube to promote products, services and happenings such as contests. I showcase events we run for clients, press conference we hold and highlights from staff retreats all on YouTube. It allows my community to look at what HJMT is doing both inside and out. It is an effective way to market and help spread your message virally.

Before you create your own videos, watch some of the more popular YouTube videos by searching "viral videos." See what the commonality is. What makes them different than other videos? Why do people send them from person to person? What would make you send a video to someone else? By answering these questions, you can make a viral video too!

Do You Have a Second Life?

"I've tried Second Life and didn't like it. I'd have to be more of a gamer to be into it."

Hilary Morris, President
H. Morris Solution

"At first, we were frustrated in our search for a location in Second Life. Once we found a business park, it worked fine for us, until we started having virtual roundtables and presentations. It was a little embarrassing because invitees often had unusual avatars. It is a bit difficult looking at a client's avatar that is an alien (from the movie of the same name) wearing a tutu and with ballerina legs. We finally retired from that world in 2008 because it was not creating much traffic among business participants—mainly hobbyists. However, it was an excellent learning experience and terrific for our marketing to be among the first law firms there."

James C. Roberts III, Esq.
Global Capital Law Group PC
California | Colorado

* * *

You've heard a lot about Second Life, but what is it really? Second Life is a virtual world in which you become a participant. You create a computerized image of someone you would like to be. Then you name the image and you become that avatar. In Second Life, you can attend virtual concerts and buy online buildings and clothing. You can also talk with other avatars and learn who they are. However, most people stay in their disguise. They don't want you to know what they do in the real world. As a matter of fact, if asked about the "real world" they will ask you what that is.

Second Life really isn't a business tool. While you may meet other Second Life avatars and perhaps even benefit from the experience, it is nearly impossible to bring those relationships into the real world.

Businesses and companies can spend a lot of money in this world, developing islands and storefronts and the like to get exposure and visibility for their products and services. However, I think there are more effective places that businesses and companies can spend their money unless they are strictly interested in the sites platform for building branding potential. But even then, it is not ideal as the sites users will have to invest a lot of time and money in ensuring they are marketing their brand in a way that will benefit them.

MY 2 CENTS

Second Life reminds me of the Sims game. People say it's a way of life, but I beg to differ. It's fun for an afternoon to explore the Second Life world and talk with people, but you really need a lot of time to fully commit to it.

I would suggest that smaller companies and non-profit organizations shy away from spending money here. Although hundreds of thousands of people are on this site, your money is better invested with blogs, podcasts and social networking sites. (Of course if you are the marketing director for a large company, you may consider buying an island or a store in Second Life.)

Non-Profit Organization's Role in Social Media

27

"When I began as CEO of Girl Scouts of Nassau County in 2000, I was pleased to see that the Council had a functioning web site. Looking back, it was probably pretty basic, but just having a website made us ahead of the curve -- then. Over the past five years, our website has become the most relied upon tool in our communication arsenal. We now use the web in so many ways to communicate directly with and among our 22,000 girls and 7,000 adult volunteers. If information is not readily available via the web, then it probably isn't happening. We have password protected web pages for each geographical group. We offer online training for adult volunteers. We use blogs and video messages. Email distribution lists enable us to communicate with targeted groups and with individuals. We publish e-newsletter on a regular basis. We do email blasts. Electronic communications give us speed and upholds our "green" values to save money and trees.

Now we are learning our way through the new maze of social networking. This is vital for Girl Scouts' business and programmatic survival. We must move at the speed of GIRLS because this is the way girls communicate. With respect to the various social media technologies – and our comfort zone – we are about where we were with our web site in 2000. However, things are moving faster than ever and we have to keep up. Sites such as Facebook allow us to both observe and interact in a somewhat less formal way with our members, weaving in Girl Scout messages in our daily comings and goings. Twitter allows us to flood a whole universe with very targeted – and succinct! – messaging. As we move toward more frequent RSS feeds and even video distribution to handheld devices, we'll keep expanding the number of people that we can reach and we will be able to reach them in the ways that they want to hear from us.

The challenge for Girl Scouts is to mobilize this technology in ways that are age-appropriate for girls and that meet the Girl Scout standards for safety and personal respect. And of course, we have to remain flexible enough to honor those adult volunteers who may not be moving as fast as the girls and the Girl Scout staff are moving."

Donna Ceravolo, CEO
Girl Scouts of Nassau County, Inc.

* * *

Social media and non-profit organizations go hand and hand. Social media allows the organization to promote its mission and reach the population it helps as well as communicate with donors via the Internet and reach a larger amount of constituents than ever before.

So why are non-profit organizations not embracing social media? In many instances, non-profits, in their quest to support a cause, are so pressed for time and resources, they are not able to pursue all of the latest avenues available to them. Still, just as with a small or large business, it is important for a non-profit organization to build a community. There are many ways to do this and I talk about this in previous chapters, but the most effective way to launch a social media campaign is to have one person or outside provider spearhead the effort. The reason to have one person launch the effort is to speak in a focused voice the community will recognize. It also helps to coordinate the massive community building effort that the non-profit organization must undertake before going forward with the social media plan. And as your organization adds more people in the community, it will better build its brand and reputation because by getting the word out to one, it will be passed along to many. By building the community properly, your organization will quickly have thousands of followers receiving information about your cause and upcoming events. Best of all, those who do implement social media campaigns find that the strategy is a great tool for driving traffic to the organization's web site, build buzz, recruit volunteers, raise money and further support their work.

Getting Followers and Friends

One of the most time consuming efforts is trying to find followers and friends within your social networking sites. Yet this is time well spent. Use it to carefully identify and select the most suitable sites and search various groups on these sites that correlate with your mission. On some of the social networking sites, like Twitter, you can even segment the market by zip code, demographics and interest using http://search.twittter.com. For example, say you have a health organization and your interested in what people are saying about the Swine Flu, go to search. twitter.com and type in Swine Flu and you will find a group of people talking about the flu.

If your board members have accounts on any of your targeted social networking sites, make sure that they help you build your community. Ask them to send out notices to their friends and followers to join your page. Also, if the organization has petitions to sign or is accepting donations, board members can send out notices to their friends and followers to support the cause.

Remember to keep up the effort. Building a community takes time and patience, but it is the best way to get your message out to the right people.

Building Awareness

Why else should a non-profit organization have a page on Facebook, Twitter, Plaxo, LinkedIn and so on?

Social networking allows the non-profit to gather a community together to help build their brand awareness and visibility for a cause. People are genuinely interested in causes and issues. They want to hear what an organization is doing and see if the charity is worth pursuing. Social networking can spread the latest news about a non-profit and its most recent achievements. Some use it to announce a new video that highlights the organization's good work, such as a newly built school or distribution of a much-needed vaccination to a third world village. What better way to inspire new supporters?

Targeting Bloggers

What is another way to gain brand awareness for your non-profit? Bloggers. Conduct an online search and identify bloggers who are interested in your position and cause. Ask them to help you by writing a story about your organization. Even when tapped by strangers, bloggers are often happy to support worthy causes. For example, people who I don't know have asked me to post stories for them on my blog, www.hilarytopper.com. Once I hear their stories and research to make sure they are legitimate, I certainly do blog about various issues.

Getting bloggers to tell your story is a great way to continue to get the word out on the Internet as potential supporters will more readily find you. Make sure that bloggers link your site to their blog. This will help you move up on the search engines on Google and Yahoo.

Real World Fundraising Efforts

By engaging an audience, non-profit organizations can help build up their fundraising efforts. For example, Charity: Water is a relatively new organization dedicated to getting water in third world countries. The organization claims on its web site that 1.1 billion people on this planet lack access to safe, clean drinking water. They give 100% of the money raised to direct project costs and ask for $20 per person. Recently, it held a global fundraising event called Twestival, which took place online and in cities across the globe. In New York City and Rochester, thousands of people came out to support the cause and meet other tweeters. To date, according to the Twestival web site (twestival.com), $250,000 was raised, helping to bring clean water to 17,000 people in Ethiopia, Uganda and India.

FeedAChild.org is another example of a non-profit organization effectively using social media. The group has more than 4.2 million fans and the web site is posted in more than a dozen languages. This global network offers sites in which visitors or fans can donate to help starving children throughout the world. The Facebook page, for example, provides photos and information about the cause and why it is important to make a donation.

Private individuals also use social media in creative ways to support causes. For instance, one woman from Austin, Texas, created a Facebook group, called American Cancer Society Benefit. She claims that if she has more than 1 million members in the group, her friend will give her a very large donation to the charity of her choice. She says she is leaning toward the American Cancer Society but is open to suggestions.

Other Strategies for Non-profits

When charities and non-profits post audio and video podcasts on the Internet about their causes, they help boost awareness and viral marketing for their brand. Supporters often also post podcasts on social networking sites, helping to spread the word about the good works of their favorite charities. In addition organizations should also consider pitching stories to online publications. Once these articles are published, organizations can better highlight their cause and at the same time improve their search engine rankings.

MY 2 CENTS

Non-profit organizations, like small and large businesses, need a strategic online marketing plan to accomplish their goals. Be sure to set a policy in your organization for users of online media. Also, have one department, preferably your PR department, handle the task of building a community and microblogging about your organization. If you don't, you can have lots of people spreading messages about your brand in different ways, making the message inconsistent and not credible. This form of viral marketing is not the kind that you as an organization want!

Media's Role in all of This...

"Social media has taken off with the general public for one good, simple reason: You can create your own personal media universe filled with people you trust and ask them for everything from expert advice to the best local Indian restaurant. It's a wakeup call to traditional media, which has moved out of the business of credibility and tried to replace it with likeability. For the traditional media to succeed now, it has to get back to the fundamental core of striving to provide the public with credible news, using multimedia that enables users to determine what's the most important news to their lives, give them the ability to delve deeper into the subject and provide meaningful feedback channels, not just reader comment ability after the story is written. Newsroom technology should be enabling reporters to talk to the public and gather information as if the reporters were walking the streets. That's not being done and the reader can see that in the generic, over processed news product currently being served up by mainstream media everywhere."

Jackie Clement, Executive Director
Fair Media Council

* * *

From the time Paul Revere made his midnight ride to President Barack Obama's election, the media has always played an important role in the lives of Americans.

Do you remember the scholar, Marshal McLuhan, who said, "The media is the message?" For the longest time, the media had the message. They had the power to persuade us to eat particular foods, wear certain clothes and vacation at specific destinations. If the media told consumers to buy a product or service, the stores could not keep up with the demands. Endorsements were aplenty.

However, rapid improvements in technology have changed the way we get our news. Technology also changes the way we digest our news. For example, does anyone under the age of 30 read a traditional print newspaper? More and more people are turning to their personal computers, laptops and even mobile devices to get information. Every day, another newspaper closes its print version, as online media grows more prevalent.

The power has shifted from the media into the hands of the consumer. Through the widespread use of the Internet, social media sites and blogs, key consumers are spreading their message and making the decisions that are affecting all of our lives. There are consumers' blogs about every subject and product imaginable and readers look to these bloggers as the experts in their fields.

Publicists and corporations used to shower reporters and producers with free gifts so that the media would try out their products. Today, bloggers get bombarded with such gifts. New restaurant owners want bloggers to come to their restaurants to enjoy a meal out and then blog about it. Savvy restaurateurs know that if dozens of bloggers write about their restaurants, people will dine there. In the movie, "Field of Dreams," Kevin Costner is told, "if you build it they will come." So rings true the power of the blogger.

Articles are now appearing in traditional media for bloggers interested in testing various products. For example, *Laptop Magazine* featured a coffee company looking for bloggers to test the coffee. When I contacted the manufacturer, it sent me various types of coffee to test out, which I did and then blogged about it.

People now communicate through social networking. Remember the 2008 Presidential campaign? President Obama is still called President 2.0 because of his savvy social media plan. He had blogs, podcasts, video podcasts, social networking sites and more to get young people out to vote for him in this historic election. Supporters helped him spread his message via viral marketing.

The Future of News Media

Although the consumer blog is important, traditional media still plays a major role in society. Some worry that there will be no offline versions of major newspapers; but I think otherwise. However, there will be fewer and fewer community newspapers and the major newspapers will become very thin, due to lack of advertising revenues.

And what about television? With the addition of digital video recorders, a vastly increasing number of people are fast-forwarding through commercials in order to get the information they want. This in turn, diminishes advertising revenue. Big corporations are learning that television advertising is not productive anymore. Today, some television shows can now be seen in full online on the station's web site. Although there are some ads online, you can fast forward through those too.

Corporations, non-profit organizations and small businesses need to be more niche centric. Advertising on blogs, forums, wikis and news media sites may prove to be the more effective and efficient way to go. By doing so, advertisers can specifically pinpoint their audience.

The Future of Public Relations

Public relations prompts people to speak with others about issues and topics. For example, someone posts a microblog and people throughout the community respond. Public Relations gets people to talk to each other to create word of mouth publicity which helps build communities. The more you talk and have comments, the more you will see your community grow.

Public Relations is changing, as people find new communities that bring them together. Take a look at Alltop.com, a site created by Guy Kawasaki. Here, you can find links to articles indexed properly and written by various authors on particular topics ranging from lifestyle and business to people and sports. This resource puts editors, reporters and bloggers at your fingertips whether you are a PR professional or a business owner doing publicity on your own.

You will also see an increasing number of PR firms creating their own newsrooms. For example, HJMT COMMUNICATIONS, LLC recently launched the HJMT Newsroom.com (www.hjmtnewsroom.com). Here, journalists can search for relevant stories and get story ideas. Instead of spamming reporters, editors and producers, we now send out short teasers via social networking sites and emails to all the targeted reporters. If they are interested, they can look on the site and get all the information they need. The site becomes more of a resource for them. They also have an opportunity to ask questions or look for other sources.

MY 2 CENTS

Since more people are turning to the web for their information, business owners need to rethink their ways of getting their message out. Consider posting releases on an online newsroom, targeting bloggers, running contests on YouTube or setting up groups on Facebook or Plaxo. The strategies of the past don't work anymore, so adapt, adjust and think of new tactics to reach your market via the Internet.

Dealing with Bad Media? Crisis Web?

"Last week, we had a real crisis situation. On Twitter someone said that there was an Airforce C17 Cargo plane that crashed in Texas. An Airforce C17 Cargo is huge, it's the size of a football field! Within 52 minutes, the story appeared on CNN Headline News, CNN.com and a bunch of other news outlets. The Airforce checked out the situation immediately and found that it was a fabrication. Paul Bove, a contractor for the Airforce and I got on Twitter and within 53 minutes squashed the story. At the end of the day, we put up a post on the Airforce blog, http://airforcelive. dodlive.mil, explaining what happened. We find social media to be an important outlet for us to talk with our public."

Capt. David Faggard, Chief of Emerging Technology
United States Airforce

*　*　*

What happens when someone writes a negative tweet about you on Twitter? Or, an angry customer posts a nasty blog about your company on his blog? What happens if these negative things go viral?

For starters, you must monitor everything about you, your company and your employees. My favorite web-monitoring tool is Google Alerts, but there are many others available. The downside: users do not receive the alerts instantaneously. Google Alerts enables me to track comments, posts and anything else where my name, company name or employees' names appear. Another great search tool is http://search.twitter.com. This enables you to search on Twitter for your company, name or anything else of interest. It will also tell you who made which comment and view their profiles on Twitter.

Once you see an angry response or something written negatively about your company, it is tempting to react. But, take it from a PR pro, don't overreact. Look at the source and think twice before responding. Consider the tone in your voice. If you want to say something, come across intelligent and not angry. Some people try to ignore it. It all depends on the situation as to whether or not you should address it.

Recently, I posted a blog on Zappos. I was angry that the company didn't get back to me in a timely manner for a quote for this book. There was certainly a misunderstanding because once I posted the blog, I received a response almost immediately from the customer service supervisor. Then I received phone calls and emails from their PR company in Boston. After I thought it was resolved, I got an apology email from Tony Hseih, the CEO of Zappos. What this tells me is that large companies like Zappos are monitoring everything on the Internet and they make sure that they try to nip the complaint right away so that it does not become viral. I was very impressed with their response to my blog post.

MY 2 CENTS

Social media is the fastest way to get your message out and heard. It goes hand and hand with crisis intervention. I believe that all businesses that are in the public eye need to be on the Internet. It is important more now than ever before to incorporate a crisis intervention plan in place, similar to what Zappos.com did with my blog post. Response to a situation is key. The U.S. Airforce was able to negate any negative publicity that was posted on Twitter about a potential disaster that didn't happen. Responsiveness is the key to addressesing any crisis or potential crisis situation.

Going Viral!

"For years, we have been trained to advertise our products and services. We have been trained to interrupt people's lives with our content. Today, things are different. If you make valuable content that is funny, inspirational or informational, people will watch. They will enjoy it and share it with their friends. That is the true meaning of going viral. It's important to strategize first and then figure out the best way to say what you want to say."

George Wright, VP Marketing and Communications
Blendtec

*   *   *

These days, everyone wants to go viral, believing that it is the best strategy to selling more products or services. This may be the case, but what it does is create a snowball effect, promoting the need for consistent messaging through many online forums. Like traditional PR, going viral means exposure and visibility throughout the Internet.

For years, we developed publicity programs that would create a snowball effect. For example, when we held an event, we would send out releases at least six to eight months prior to the event and then every month thereafter. A month before the event, we sent out information weekly. This would generate coverage from the media.

Today, going viral means ensuring that a product or service appears on the Internet in many different places including blogs, podcasts, video podcasts and social networking sites.

What makes something go viral? It is the reblogging, the sending of podcasts and video podcasts to your community and the forwarding of information from social networking sites. Going viral also means that people put your blog or information in a social bookmarketing spot and share it with others. Soon, hundreds of thousands of people read about your company and get excited about your company's offerings.

Burger King is a great example. They came up with the idea of marketing the aroma of the flame-broiled burger as a men's cologne. They launched the cologne in December 2008. Within weeks, they sold out and after that the cologne was only available on EBay for no less than $20, when it originally sold for $3.99. Bloggers, online journalists and social networking people all wrote about this cologne posting links to the product. Whether or not they thought it was a good idea didn't matter. Their action created demand.

About a month later, Burger King announced on Facebook that if you de-friend 10 friends on Facebook, then you would receive a free Whopper. Why? They wanted to see how much their supporters loved Whoppers. Thousands of people took

Burger King up on their offer and received coupons for a free whopper. It didn't take long. One person saw it, blogged about it, tweeted about it on Twitter, sending the information out to a whole group who sent it out to their community and so on and so on. That's what viral marketing is all about.

Another good example of a product going viral is the Snuggie blanket. Commercials on television were abundant. On my blog, someone posted that the marketing people bought up ads on television when there was a lot of airtime inventory so that they got these commercials for less than normal. I'm not sure if that is the case or not. But what I am sure about is that this product went viral. How did that happen? The company sent out multiple emails many different times to the same audience. (I received 50 over a two-week period.) Soon, bloggers, like myself either started to either get annoyed or recommend the product. The next thing we all knew, the product had one of the highest blogger ratings. People also began to Twitter about it and this in turn helped the product go viral. Bill Mahr even wore the Snuggie on his HBO show, *Real Time*. There were even reports of a Snuggie Bar Crawl taking place in Manhattan by Snuggie fanatics.

MY 2 CENTS

On Donald Trump's Celebrity Apprentice (NBC-Sunday evenings), the two groups were asked to make a viral video for the laundry detergent ALL. I was surprised by what the groups came up with because both groups had incredibly creative people. Both were inappropriate videos that would not go viral. Going viral doesn't have to include bathroom humor or sexual innuendos. It should strike an emotion, whether it's laughter, crying or just plain joy, when watching the video. Blendtec, Burger King, Snuggie are all good examples of products and services going viral.

Where Do We Go From Here? Web 3.0...

"Hilary, I don't know what any of this is – it sounds like a script for a Star Trek episode! I am still trying to figure out the ground rules on many, many aspects of Facebook and LinkedIn and how to use social media effectively. The whole thing changes so fast and can be such a time suck. PR and marketing people are feeding Facebook one minute, twittering the next, digging, squidooing, blogging, etc. Does anybody do any work any more?"

Anne Sweeney, Writer and Publicist

* * *

Once your marketing plan includes social media, it's time to move forward with it. Social media is constantly changing and evolving. This is something to keep in mind when marketing your business and setting yourself apart from competitors.

It is important to be responsive to current trends. Right now, the direction is to go smaller and portable and to be wired

24/7. Just look at our children holding their Nintendo DS or our friends using cell phones for Internet access and text messaging. Soon you will see Blackberry's and other mobile devices including laptops that are smaller, quicker and smarter. Everything will be available at our fingertips and people will be "plugged in" 24/7.

Video blogging will become bigger than ever before. Politicians, school superintendents, marketers and business owners will all soon send video messages. You may even be able to use your iPhone or Blackberry to relay video messages instead of text messages. It's already happening. Stay current with these trends to help your business continue to grow and prosper.

In Conclusion

As discussed, there are hundreds of social networking sites online. There are thousands of blog and microblog sites. And there are tons of sites for podcasts and video podcasts. Spend some time on the sites where your community gravitates and understand how to tie them all together to promote your product or service. This is how you will get a sense of the direction we are heading towards in terms of communication. Yes, initially, the various sites and applications seem confusing. And yet, when executed properly, they can be used to help your business grow in a cost effective manner.

MY FINAL 2 CENTS

So here's my advice – if you only have a small amount of time to devote to social media, focus on three or four popular sites. Get to really understand these sites and start using them to build your community. Set up a company blog or guest blog on related blogs or both. Most importantly, remember to continue your social media efforts. With consistency, you will see results.

As you can see, we've come a long way from black and white televisions and dial phones. The future holds so many endless possibilities and by keeping up with the technology, you will be ahead of the curve. Enjoy surfing!

Acknowledgements

There are a lot of people that I would like to thank for their help and support with this book. First and foremost, I want to thank my family for allowing me to write in the middle of the night, on vacation and during our favorite television shows during family hour.

I also want to thank my staff at HJMT COMMUNICATIONS, LLC who helped with research, proofing and designing the cover of this book. Thanks for holding the reins for me occasionally while I wrote and edited the book.

Also, a big thank you to my community – all of my followers on Twitter, my friends on Facebook, my contacts on LinkedIn, Plaxo, Seesmic and so on. I greatly value your insights and learn from you every day.

Author's Bio

Hilary JM Topper, MPA, has nearly 30 years of public relations, advertising and marketing experience. In March 1992, Hilary founded HJMT COMMUNICATIONS, LLC, a boutique Public Relations, Social Media, Event Planning & Graphic Design Agency.

Prior to HJMT COMMUNICATIONS, LLC, Hilary was the Director of Public Relations and Development at Professional Service Centers for the Handicapped, Inc. (P.S.C.H.). In 1989, Hilary Topper joined Ruder Finn Public Relations where she was the account executive for Jell-O and GLAD Wrap Bags. She represented clients on broadcast media and implemented a grass root fundraising campaign in local markets.

Prior to that, Hilary was the Director of Public Affairs at Altro Health and Rehabilitation Services. She was responsible for all the day-to-day public relations, marketing and fundraising activities. In 1985, Hilary worked at Hill, Holliday, Connors, Cosmopulos, Inc., Public Relations as an account executive. There, she handled the PRESTONE II antifreeze account, coordinating a national radio promotion. In addition, she managed The National Community Gardening Contest, sponsored by the American Community Gardening Association. She also trained spokespeople for media and placed them on national and regional television.

Prior to that, Hilary worked at Ogilvy & Mather Public Relations. There, she worked on Dove Beauty Bar, Quadro (a children's construction kit) and Kinder-Care Learning Centers, Inc. Hilary wrote press releases, pitch letters and booked media tours in local markets. Before that, she worked at CLAIROL, Inc. publicizing hair care products and at Public I Publicity, promoting musicians and music books.

Hilary has received numerous awards and honors for her accomplishments within the industry from *PRWeek, Long Island Business News, Newsday,* Girl Scouts of Nassau County, the Communicator, International Association of Business Communicators, Long Island Center for Business and Professional Women, Diversity Business.com and the Stevie Awards.

She is a published author and has given numerous speeches and seminars across the country. She is a blogger, entrepreneur and mother of two. Hilary received her Bachelor of Science degree from Hunter College and her Masters in Public Administration from Baruch College.